Gary E. McCuen

IDEAS IN CONFLICT SERIES

publications inc.

411 Mallalieu Drive
Hudson, Wisconsin 54016

Illustration & photo credits
American Lutheran Church 71, Bread for the World 24, British Anti-Apartheid Movement 146, CALC Report 21, 34, 59, 65, 112, Yuri Cherepanov 97, E. Gentry 78, Ollie Harrington 43, Charles Keller 159, S. Kelly 102, Tom Keough 84, The Militant 118, Sack 134, Sanders 170, South African Government 90, South African Panorama 53, 106, 124, 165, Survey 10, 14, Wright 129

© 1986 by Gary E. McCuen Publications, Inc.
411 Mallalieu Drive • Hudson, Wisconsin 54016
(715) 386-5662
International Standard Book Number 0-86596-057-7
Printed in the United States of America

CONTENTS

CHAPTER 3 CORPORATE DIVESTMENT

CHAPTER 4 THE U.S. AND SOUTH AFRICA

REASONING SKILL DEVELOPMENT

These activities may be used as individualized study guides for students in libraries and resource centers or as discussion catalysts in small group and classroom discussions.

IDEAS in CONFLICT®

This series features ideas in conflict on political, social and moral issues. It presents counterpoints, debates, opinions, commentary and analysis for use in libraries and classrooms. Each title in the series uses one or more of the following basic elements:

Introductions that present an issue overview giving historic background and/or a description of the controversy.

Counterpoints and debates carefully chosen from publications, books, and position papers on the political right and left to help librarians and teachers respond to requests that treatment of public issues be fair and balanced.

Symposiums and forums that go beyond debates that can polarize and oversimplify. These present commentary from across the political spectrum that reflect how complex issues attract many shades of opinion.

A global emphasis with foreign perspectives and surveys on various moral questions and political issues that will help readers to place subject matter in a less culture-bound and ethno-centric frame of reference. In an ever shrinking and interdependent world, understanding and cooperation are essential. Many issues are global in nature and can be effectively dealt with only by common efforts and international understanding.

Reasoning skill study guides and discussion activities provide ready made tools for helping with critical reading and evaluation of content. The guides and activities deal with one or more of the following:

RECOGNIZING AUTHOR'S POINT OF VIEW

INTERPRETING EDITORIAL CARTOONS

VALUES IN CONFLICT

WHAT IS EDITORIAL BIAS?

WHAT IS SEX BIAS?
WHAT IS POLITICAL BIAS?
WHAT IS ETHNOCENTRIC BIAS?
WHAT IS RACE BIAS?
WHAT IS RELIGIOUS BIAS?

*From across **the political spectrum** varied sources are presented for research projects and classroom discussions. Diverse opinions in the series come from magazines, newspapers, syndicated columnists, books, political speeches, foreign nations, and position papers by corporations and non-profit institutions.*

About the Editor

Gary E. McCuen is an editor and publisher of anthologies for public libraries and curriculum materials for schools. Over the past 16 years his publications of over 200 titles have specialized in social, moral and political conflict. They include books, pamphlets, cassettes, tabloids, filmstrips and simulation games, many of them designed from his curriculums during 11 years of teaching junior and senior high school social studies. At present he is the editor and publisher of the *Ideas in Conflict* series and the *Editorial Forum* series.

CHAPTER 1

REALITIES OF APARTHEID

1   THE APARTHEID SYSTEM
    The Africa Fund

2   SEPARATE DEVELOPMENT
    International Labour Office

3   THE TRIBAL HOMELANDS
    *Lawyers' Committee for Civil Rights
    Under Law*

4   HUNGER IN THE HOMELANDS
    Jan Pager

5   HEALTH CARE UNDER APARTHEID
    Pippa Gordon

6   WOMEN UNDER APARTHEID
    Margaret Mackay

7   CHILDREN UNDER APARTHEID
    International Defence and Aid Fund

8   THE TORTURE AND TERROR:
    ENFORCING APARTHEID
    Gay J. McDougall

    **Case Study on Torture:
    A Tale of Hope and Despair**
    Paul Levy

1 REALITIES OF APARTHEID

THE APARTHEID SYSTEM

The Africa Fund

Twenty-nine million people live in South Africa today. Only the 4.5 million whites have full rights of citizenship while the nation's twenty-one million Africans are treated as rightless foreigners. The Africans were born in South Africa, work in South Africa, and will die in South Africa—but they are black and under South African law, the color of their skin makes them non-citizens. Africans cannot vote, buy or sell land, live or work where they choose, or move freely. They have been stripped of power and deprived of control over their lives by an elaborate network of legislation and custom.

This is the apartheid system. A rising tide of black opposition is today threatening the survival of apartheid. The racist government is responding with violence at home and false propaganda abroad in its efforts to save the system.

This fact sheet is designed to present an accurate picture of the continuing impact apartheid has on the lives of black people in South Africa today.

Reprinted from "South Africa Fact Sheet," January, 1984, a newsletter by The Africa Fund, an organization assisting African peoples struggling for independence.

Land

Area: 472,359 square miles (larger than California, Arizona, Utah and Nevada combined). Yearbook, 1979.

Land Reservation: Under the Land Acts of 1913 and 1936, 87% of the country's territory has been reserved for whites, 13% for Africans. Africans may not purchase land in white areas and may not remain in the white areas without a permit. Indians and Coloureds must live in segregated areas in the territory reserved for whites.

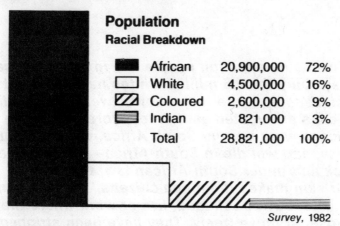

Population
Racial Breakdown

■	African	20,900,000	72%
☐	White	4,500,000	16%
▨	Coloured	2,600,000	9%
▤	Indian	821,000	3%
	Total	28,821,000	100%

Survey, 1982

The Bantustans: The fragmented areas designated for Africans are called bantustans, homelands or national states. As of 1983 fewer than 10,000,000 Africans, or 46% of the African population, lived in white areas and more than 11,000,000, or 54%, lived in the bantustans. Of ten designated bantustans, the white government has implemented 'independence' for the Transkei, Bophuthatswana, Venda and Ciskei, but this status has not been recognized by the United Nations or by any country. SA Review, 1983.

Forced Removals: Since 1960, the South African government has removed 3,500,000 blacks from white areas to areas designated for blacks. At least one million more Africans have been forcibly relocated within the bantustans. A further 1,700,000 people are under threat of removal. SPP.

Government

The South Africa Act of 1909 and the Republic of South Africa Act of 1961 restricted voting for and membership in the governing parliament to whites. In November, 1983, white voters endorsed a new constitution which will establish a tricameral parliament with separate chambers for whites, Coloureds, and Indians. Whites retain a monopoly of real power and the African majority is totally excluded. Black political organizations and independent trade unions, as well as the Organization of African Unity and the United Nations, have rejected this racial constitutional reform.

Income and Employment

Migrant Labor, 1981: 1,329,000 Africans from the ten bantustans were working in white areas as migrant laborers under contract, a system which forces the separation of workers from their families. Also, 301,758 foreign blacks were employed as contract laborers in South Africa. Survey, 1982.

Commuters, 1981: 745,500 Africans were employed in white areas but forced to live in the bantustans and commute to work on a daily basis. Survey, 1982.

Agriculture: An estimated 1.3 million people work on white owned farms. In 1980 the average wage for African farmworkers was $28 to $40 per month. Farmworkers also receive "in kind" payment such as minimal housing facilities and the dietary staple corn, or "mealie" meal. Farm Labour Project, Sept. 1982.

Employment and Average Monthly Wages:

Mining, May 1983	# Employed	Av Monthly Wage
African	613,452	$260
White	78,020	$1,395
Coloured	9,581	$430
Indian	659	$690

Manufacturing, May 1983		
African	748,700	$320
White	326,600	$1,290
Coloured	240,800	$365
Indian	86,400	$460

Central Statistical Services.

Domestic Workers: An estimated 700,000 people, primarily women, are employed as domestic servants. Salaries commonly range from $40 to $80 a month, but are frequently lower. ICFTU, June, 1983; Survey, 1982.

African Income vs. Poverty Level: In 1980 the estimated percentages of African households in major urban areas with incomes below the Household Subsistence Level (HSL) were: Johannesburg (62%); Pretoria (58%); Durban (65%); Port Elizabeth (70%). The HSL estimates the minimum income necessary for the subsistence of an African family of six including food and rent but excluding medical and educational cost. In 1983, in the 13 largest urban centers, the Household Subsistence Level ranged from $243 to $268 for an African family. While cash wages have been increasing, researchers indicate that in real terms Africans' wages are decreasing. FM Nov. 25, 1983, Survey, 1980/82.

African Unemployment: The government estimated African unemployment at 7.8% in June 1981. Others have estimated African unemployment to be considerably higher, up to 25% or two to three million people. Survey 1982.

Education

Attendance: All public education is racially segregated with racially differentiated curricula. In 1982, of the 3,708,000 African students in school, 83% were in the primary grades, 16% in secondary, and 2% reached the post high school level. Of the 1,283,000 white students, 55% were in primary, 30% in secondary, and 15% in the post high school level. Nedbank, 1983.

Per Capita Spending on Education, 1980/81: Whites—$1,115; Africans—$170; Coloureds—$310; Indians—$625. Survey, 1982.

Teacher/Pupil Ratios, 1982: Whites—1:18; Africans—1:39; Coloureds—1:27; Indians—1:24. Survey, 1982.

Health

Mortality: In 1980, the infant mortality rates per 1000 live births were 13 for whites, 24 for Indians, 62 for Coloureds and 90 for Africans. In some rural areas, mortality rates for Africans are much higher with estimates of 220 per 1,000 to

320 per 1,000. Life expectancy for white men was 67 years; for African men, 55 years; for white women, 74 years; for African women 60 years. Nedbank, 1983.

Malnutrition: Conservative estimates show that 2.9 million black children under the age of 15 suffer from malnutrition. Star May 14, 1933.

Doctor/Patient Ratios: Whites—1:330; Africans—1:19,000; Coloureds—1:12,000; Indians—1:730. Rand Daily Mail, Dec. 14, 1983.

U.S.—South Africa Economic Ties

U.S. Companies Doing Business in South Africa, 1982: More than 350 U.S. companies have subsidiaries in South Africa. Time Running Out.

U.S. Percentage of Total Foreign Direct Investment in South Africa: Approximately 20%. (U.S. investment is second only to that of Britain.) Time Running Out.

Average Rate of Return on U.S. Investment: Between 1979 and 1982, 18.7%, compared to an average rate of return for U.S. companies worldwide of 16%. Calculations from Survey CB, August 1979 through 1983.

Major U.S. Corporate Operations in South Africa: Direct investments—Mobil Oil ($426 million/3,577 workers); Caltex [Standard Oil of California and Texaco] ($334 million/2,238 workers); General Motors ($243 million/5,038 workers); Goodyear ($97 million/2,797 workers); Union Carbide ($54.5 million/2,465 workers); SOHIO [Kennecott] ($345 million/2,259 workers). Ford ($213 million/6,509 workers); Newmont ($127 million/13,535 workers; General Electric ($93 million/5,130 workers). Other involvement—Fluor ($4.7 billion contract for oil from coal facility/17,300 workers); Burroughs Corp. ($6 million annual sales/558 workers); Control Data Corporation ($17.8 million annual sales/330 workers); IBM ($262 million annual sales/1,800 workers). Unified List.

U.S. Bank Loans to South Africa: As of June, 1983 loans outstanding from U.S. banks totalled $3.88 billion. More than 125 U.S. banks have made loans to government and private borrowers in recent years. Among the significant lenders have been: Bankers Trust (NY), BankAmerica (CA), Chase Manhattan (NY), Chemical Bank (NY), Citibank (NY), Continental Illinois (IL), First Boston (MA), First Chicago (IL),

Manufacturers Hanover (NY), Morgan Guaranty (NY). USFRB,
Nov. 17, 1983; Unified List.

US Financial Involvement in South Africa, 1982:

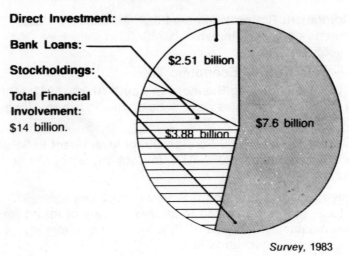

Direct Investment:

Bank Loans:

Stockholdings:

Total Financial
Involvement:
$14 billion.

$2.51 billion

$3.88 billion

$7.6 billion

Survey, 1983

Repression and Control

Legislation: The Internal Security Act of 1982 consolidates a
series of laws, including the Terrorism Act, and Unlawful
Organization Act and the General Laws Amendment Act,
with minor revisions, into one law. This act allows: 1)
indefinite incommunicado detention without charge or trial;
2) the outlawing of any organization alleged to be threatening to public safety or order; 3) the prohibition of the print-
ing, publication or dissemination of any periodical or any
other publication; 4) the prohibition of any gathering or
meeting; 5) random police searches; 6) the curtailment of
travel rights of any person, and restriction of rights of communication, association and participation in any activity
(banning). Further, it is illegal under this act to render any
assistance to any campaign, at home or abroad, that protests or seeks to modify or repeal any law if such a campaign furthers the aims of a banned organization.

The Pass Act applies only to Africans and is the key to the administration of apartheid and labor control: all Africans over age 16 are required to be fingerprinted and carry a pass book at all times with a record of bantustan identification, employment, permits to enter white areas, taxes and family status.

The National Key Points Act empowers the Minister of Defense to declare any place or area a National Key Point and requires the owner to provide security in cooperation with the South African Defense Force. These provisions can be applied to any U.S. corporation operating in South Africa. It is illegal under this act to print any information about security measures or any incident at a National Key Point without permission from the government.

Official Violence: The State has consistently sanctioned a high level of violence in repressing opposition to apartheid. Over the years, thousands of peaceful demonstrators have been shot by police. Sixty-nine people died at Sharpeville in 1960 and at least 575 people died in 1976 during and after the Soweto uprising according to official statistics. Foreign Affairs, Haysom.

Detention Without Trial: From Jan. 1 to August 31, 1983, 306 people are known to have been held incommunicado, mainly in terms of Section 29 of the Internal Security Act. At least 67 more were held under Ciskei's Internal Security Act. Since 1963, 59 people are known to have died while being detained by the security police. FM Nov. 4, 1983, Haysom, Lawyers Committee.

Torture: Torture is extensively inflicted on political detainees by both South African and bantustan security police. Methods used include electric shock, beatings, sleep deprivation and isolation. AI; DPSS, Sept. 30, 1982.

Prison Population: South Africa has the highest per capita prison population in the world with 440 people jailed for every 100,000 of the population. The equivalent figure for the U.S. is 189. 40% of the African prison population consists of people convicted of pass law violations, "crimes" only Africans can commit. Sunday Times, April 12, 1981.

Hanging: Of the 130 people hanged in South Africa in 1980, only one was white. Update, Jan. 1983.

REALITIES OF APARTHEID

SEPARATE DEVELOPMENT

International Labour Office

Any consideration of the problem of apartheid must be set within the human context of the South African scene. South Africa is a multi-racial country. According to the 1980 census, its population was estimated to be composed of about 20.8 million Blacks, 4.5 million Whites, 2.6 million Coloured (i.e. of mixed racial origin) and just over 800,000 Asians. The Black population is made up of several related ethnic groups. The Whites are descended mainly from Dutch, British, French and German settlers and are divided into two main groups—about 60 percent speaking Afrikaans (a language derived from Dutch) and 40 percent speaking English. The majority of the Coloured people live in Western Cape Province. The Asians are mainly descendants of Indians who were brought over to work as labourers on sugar plantations in the nineteenth century and live predominantly in the province of Natal.

From a Colour Policy to "Separate Development"

From the time of the first Dutch settlement at the Cape of Good Hope in the middle of the seventeenth century, the Whites progressively extended their rule over the whole of the present territory of South Africa, which when so occupied was lightly populated. This process was accelerated in the nineteenth century when a large part of the Dutch settlers migrated into the interior to escape British rule, and settled in parts of Natal and what are now the Orange Free State and Transvaal, while English settlers also

Excerpted from *Apartheid and Labour,* International Labour Office (Geneva, 1983) pp.9-13.

moved into the eastern Cape and Natal. As the Whites came increasingly into contact with the Black peoples, they were able to subdue the latter owing to their superior military force and more sophisticated form of society.

The discovery, towards the end of the nineteenth century, of considerable mineral wealth, which eventually led to the urban and industrial expansion which characterizes modern South Africa, made necessary the availability of a large labour force to develop these resources; much of this was attracted from further north, largely by economic opportunity. There thus developed a form of master and servant relationship in which the Whites controlled all the levers of political and economic command while the Blacks supplied the basic labour force needed both in the mines and on the white farms. The pervading inequality to which this gave rise remains at the root of the present situation in South Africa. This pattern was extended through legislation to the growing industrial sector, and applied as well to fields involving industrial relations and labour, particularly in the first two decades after the establishment of the Union of South Africa in 1910. With the advent to power in 1948 of the National Party, which has ruled South Africa ever since, racial discrimination has been further entrenched by a systematic application of the Government's policy.

Systematic Legal Discrimination

While cases of racial discrimination occur in other parts of the world, it is the systematic official and legalistic character of apartheid which makes South Africa unique in the world today. Whereas other multi-racial countries accept the principle of racial equality and seek to guarantee equal rights for all their citizens, South Africa alone deliberately continues to pursue a policy which denies racial equality and seeks to bring about the separation of the racial groups. This policy has been applied by all methods of action at the disposal of the South African Government, in particular by the adoption of an extensive network of laws concerning every aspect of human activity.

The cornerstone of this policy is the system of race classification introduced by the Population Registration Act, 1950, under which the whole population is classified into a number of rigid racial categories. It is a person's racial classification and not his individual merits or qualifications which determines what rights he may exercise. It is clear that this system also has decisive consequences in the labour field, since the policy and law are that a person's racial category determines what education and training he will receive and the scope of his employment opportunities. At the same time as it multiplied legislation on the statute-book restricting the rights of the non-White population, the Government pushed ahead with its plans to bring about a physical separation of the races to the maximum extent to forestall the consequences which the increasing interdependence of the races in the economic life of South Africa might have in terms of general racial integration. The policy officially known as "separate development" is aimed at dividing South Africa into a territorial unit reserved for White control and ten areas set aside for Blacks, established on an ethnic basis and referred to as "homelands". The area controlled by the Whites (about 20 percent of the population) amounts to 87 percent of the whole territory of the Republic, including all the main urban and industrial areas, whereas the Blacks (about 70 percent of the population) are only to occupy 13 percent of the national territory. As regards the "White areas", the Government's intention has clearly been stated as being that "for all eternity, as long as we exercise the authority, we stand for the domination of the Whites in the White areas". The theory behind the concept of "separate development" is that Blacks will be allowed to exercise their normal political, economic and social rights in the areas reserved for them. However, in practice, the policy results in millions of Blacks living and working permanently in the "White areas" and, although often having only the remotest connection with their areas of ethnic origin in addition to being deprived of the most basic rights, they are increasingly reduced to the status of aliens within their own country by loss of citizenship brought about by the so-called "independence" of their "homelands". This situation will be perpetuated since the White economy is now highly dependent on Black labour; but the policy of the South African Government is to maintain the number of Blacks in White areas at the level of the economy's general needs, with any additional labour requirements met by Blacks from the "homelands" on a short-term migratory basis and as single men. The emphasis in this policy of "separate development" has been on political separation quite as much as on territorial separation. Whereas at first apartheid deprived the Black of his rights in the White areas because he was destined to develop elsewhere, now this absence of rights is invoked to suggest that politically the Black is not there, even if physically and economically he is present in the White areas. While the White economy's labour needs have forced the Government to adjust its utilization of Black labour policies in recent years, the official attitude to Black labour remains that expressed by a National Party MP who argued that:

"Just as someone overseas who sells machinery to us is supplying a commodity, so the Black labourer is supplying a commodity to us, but that does not mean that we are integrating them into our economy as individuals. . . .As soon as the Opposition understands this principle that it is labour we are importing, and not labourers as individuals, the question of numbers will no longer worry them either."

The linchpin in this policy is the influx control system which seeks to maintain Black workers as an alien and migratory labour force without roots or rights in the White areas.

REALITIES OF APARTHEID

THE TRIBAL HOMELANDS

Lawyers' Committee for Civil Rights Under Law

Official South African government policy has the entire black population allocated to ten tribal homelands (bantustans)—a total area of 14 percent of South Africa's land—despite the fact that the vast majority do not live there and have expressed no desire to be identified with those territories. The 1980 census in South Africa recorded 19.8 million Africans, of which 9.5 million or 48% were officially recorded as residing in the "white" areas and 10.3 million or 52% as residing in the homelands. These figures are highly unreliable. According to Barbara Rogers: So many Africans are present in urban areas without authorization that the urban population is seriously undercounted; and many of those in the bantustans would have their reasons, such as fear of taxation, to give distorted information. . . .Official ideology has the entire African population allocated to one or other of the bantustans, despite the fact that the majority have never lived there (and probably a larger majority than the official figures indicate). The result is the rather bizarre situation where for most of the bantustans, and for the group as a whole, more than half the people allocated to them on paper have no connections there. In official terms, the *de facto* population is less than half the *de jure* population.[1] Under the terms of the Bantu Homelands Citizenship

Reprinted from "The Commission of Inquiry into KaNgwane, Lawyers' Committee for Civil Rights Under Law (Washington, March 13, 1984) pp. 2-5

[1] B. Rodgers, *D.I.V.I.D.E. and Rule: South Africa's Bantustans,* 35 (2d ed. 1980).

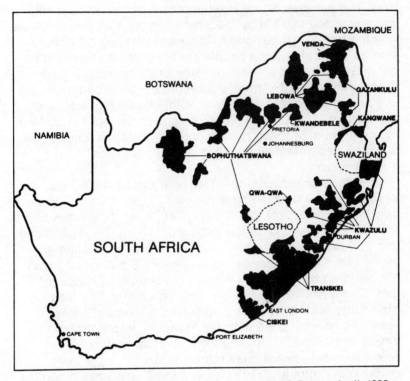

CALC Report, April, 1985

Act (now the National States Citizenship Act), every African was designated a citizen of a "homeland" on the basis of language, birth, or cultural affiliation. The identity document which all Blacks are required to carry is marked with the person's official tribal classification, homeland citizenship, personal records, and fingerprints. "Pass laws" restrict Blacks to the homelands except for those needed for work in the non-homeland areas that are generally designated as "white" areas.

The Bantustans

The bantustans, where the population density is approximately 120 per square mile, are not economically viable. Yet, the government policy is to separate by law the bantustans from South Africa by declaring them "independent" countries. The purpose of the establishment of the bantustans was explained in 1978 by the South African Minister of Bantu Administration: "If our policy is taken to its logical conclusion as far as the Black people are concerned, there will be not one Black man with South African citizenship. . .Every Black man in South Africa will eventually be accommodated in some independent new state in this honorable way and there will no longer be a moral obligation on this Parliament to accommodate these people politically." Thus, clearly the policy of separate development is based on racial discrimination.

To date, four bantustans—Transkei, BophuthaTswana, Venda, and the Ciskei—have become "independent." They now have a president, parliament, flag, even a diplomatic service. However, no nation but South Africa has recognized this purported accession to statehood. The practical meaning of this "independence" is that nearly 8 million Africans are declared by the South African government to have lost their South African citizenship and nationality. The loss of nationality occurs when the homeland becomes "independent," as was the case with the Transkei, BophuthaTswana, Venda, and Ciskei. Thus, the South African policy of separate development has created distinctions between citizenship rights and nationality. John Dugard has made the following analysis: "The present situation can be summarized in the following way: all white, colored or Indian South Africans are South African nationals. Similarly, all black South Africans who are not ethnically connected with Transkei, BophuthaTswana, or Venda are South African nationals. Within South Africa there are, however, different types of citizens: those who exercise political rights in the central political process (Whites); those whom the government plans to incorporate into the central political process (Coloreds and Indians); and those who have political rights in the nonindependent homelands (Blacks). From this it will be seen that nationality is a wider concept than citizenship. All South Africans are South African nationals, but blacks and Whites enjoy different citizenship rights."[2] Africans whose citizenship is allocated to the bantustans are now said to have "guest worker" status in South Africa.

[2] J. Dugard, South Africa's "Independent" Homelands: An Exercise in Denationalization, 10 Den. J. of Int'l L. Pol'y II, 22 (1980).

REALITIES OF APARTHEID

HUNGER IN THE HOMELANDS

Jan Pager

Southern Africa has always been a semi-arid region, and severe droughts recur there regularly. But before the late 19th century imposition of colonial rule in the interior, subsistence farmers were able to move relatively freely to escape drought. Today, private land ownership and international borders block farmers' movements, and poor farmers who cannot afford irrigation systems can do little more than watch as their fields dry up.

This year's drought appears to be part of a cyclical climate pattern and may well be the first of several dry years. But in this part of the world, it is hard to ignore the social aspect of natural disasters: inevitably, it is the rural poor who will be hardest hit.

Urban dwellers throughout the region will be affected by the drought too. In South Africa, food prices for basic staples are expected to rise 15 percent this month, and electricity and water will be in short supply. This winter will not be easy for anyone without a steady income.

But in rural areas, where many farmers have harvested less than 10 percent of their normal crop, the drought's impact will be more direct. Farmers who cannot afford feed for cattle are already slaughtering their herds rather than watching them starve—or selling them at low prices to wealthier neighbors who can afford feed. Rural women—who in this part of the world are largely responsible for fetching water—will spend many more hours with buckets on their heads, searching for rivers that have not yet dried up. And of

Reprinted from Jan Pager, "Drought, Famine Fall Heavily on Rural Black Majority," *In These Times*, July 27-August 9, 1983, p.8.

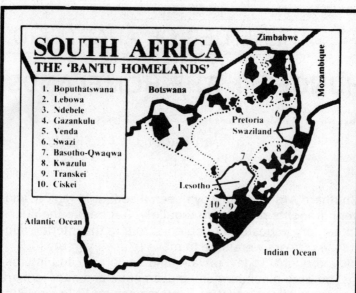

SOUTH AFRICA
THE 'BANTU HOMELANDS'

1. Boputhatswana
2. Lebowa
3. Ndebele
4. Gazankulu
5. Venda
6. Swazi
7. Basotho-Qwaqwa
8. Kwazulu
9. Transkei
10. Ciskei

Zimbabwe

Mozambique

Botswana

Pretoria
Swaziland

Lesotho

Atlantic Ocean

Indian Ocean

Land and Hunger: South Africa

In South Africa, rigid control of the land by whites is the major cause of poverty for the country's 23 million black people. Segregated into "homelands" or *bantustans* by the country's apartheid system, blacks, who make up 70 percent of the population, hold 13 percent of the land. Observant travelers flying over South Africa report that it is easy to tell from the air which land is "white" and which is "black." The poor, arid, infertile land of the *bantustans* sticks out like gray-brown blotches on a green, fertile landscape. Unlike other African regions, South Africa was heavily settled and farmed by white European colonists, who found the climate hospitable. The system their descendants maintain impoverishes millions of people in the continent's wealthiest country.

Source: Bread for the World

course, poorer farmers will find it difficult to get cash for food and other necessities.

The pattern is hardly unique to southern Africa. The World Bank's 1982 Development Report says, "Rarely. . .does famine result from a reduction in food production and affect all people in the area uniformly. Major groups of the poor, especially the landless, [are] extremely vulnerable to a sudden reduction in their earnings. In such cases, and particularly if prices rise suddenly, these are the people who starve."

But the disparity in the effects of drought are particularly evident in South Africa, where the apartheid system has allocated about 13 percent of the land area to the 70 percent of the population that is black.

Even at the best of times, infant mortality rates among rural black South Africans rise to 50 percent. This winter, a child will die in the black-designated bantustans every three hours from malnutrition.

The justification for apartheid is "separate development": blacks are supposed to be able to grow enough food in the bantustans to feed themselves. Even in the best of times, however, families crowded onto dry and infertile farmland only survive because of remittances from family members who go off to work in white-owned industrial South Africa.

This winter, looking down from a small plane flying over South Africa, you can see the results of "separate development." It is easy during the drought to tell which fields are white-owned and which are in bantustans—the large, well-irrigated white-owned fields stand in stark contrast to the small dry plots of the bantustans.

Failed harvests mean that rural black South Africans—restricted from moving to the cities by South Africa's infamous pass laws—must rely completely on migrant laborers' remittances. Yet this reliance underlines the Catch-22 in which many South African families are trapped: migrant laborers are rarely paid much more than is needed to support a single man, since laborers' wages are only meant to supplement agricultural production in the bantustans.

A recent report on migrant labor issued by the main workers recruiting organization argued that this year's drought highlights a positive aspect of the migrant system. Remittances, the report argues, will keep rural families alive through the winter—an argument that cynically ignores the role that "pass" laws play in restricting blacks to impoverished rural areas.

The pass laws—euphemistically called "influx control"—are designed to stop blacks from moving to white-designated cities unless they are employed. A recent court

> # Malnutrition
>
> *Malnutrition, even slow starvation, is found in the so-called homelands—barren land where millions have been compelled to resettle. Chronic gastroenteritis, malaria, typhoid fever and cholera are widespread. Tuberculosis, virtually eradicated among whites, occurs at the rate of 285 cases per 100,000 blacks.*
>
> Robert Coles, *Minneapolis Star and Tribune*, February 17, 1985.

decision could give migrant laborers the right to permanent urban residence, but even so, the government appears unwilling to allow their families to join them.

Food as Political Weapon

Not surprisingly, given the extent of the drought, emergency food aid is quickly turning into a political weapon throughout southern Africa. In Zimbabwe, government officials have threatened to withdraw food aid from villages suspected of harboring "dissidents." Socialist Mozambique, where four million people could starve this winter, is finding it difficult to persuade Western countries to donate food supplies to ward off famine.

And in South Africa, bantustan "leaders" who have accepted nominal independence from Pretoria—"leaders" who have been repeatedly denounced as corrupt and repressive by the people they are supposed to rule—have found they can use food aid to force people to accept their rule. In the recently "independent" Ciskei, for example—an area whose main product, like the main products of most of the bantustans, is cheap labor—bags of desperately needed corn flour (the staple food in southern Africa) are rotting in warehouses. Only card-carrying members of President-for-Life Lennox Sebe's Ciskei National Independence Party can get aid.

Joining Sebe's party means accepting the principle that blacks will no longer be considered citizens of South Africa, and as non-citizens, will have no rights in most of the country—except, of course, the right to work as migrant labor.

It is not unusual for bantustan leaders to link social services—health, education or even passes for migrant laborers—to their party membership. But during this drought, the depth of their cynicism becomes even clearer.

Like its bantustan-leader puppets, Pretoria seems likely to use the drought as yet another club over its neighbors. Already heavily dependent on South Africa's industries and transportation networks, the majority-ruled countries surrounding South Africa may find it difficult to act against Pretoria's wishes this winter.

Botswana, long one of the frontline states most supportive of the liberation movement, is in a particularly weak position during the drought. Half its population of about one million is already receiving food aid, and the country now depends on South Africa for all its electricity.

This winter, South Africa may not have to use military force to keep its neighbors from supporting the liberation movement's efforts. As leaders of Botswana, Mozambique, Zimbabwe and other majority-ruled southern African countries pointed out at a conference held in Maputo in July, South Africa's economic hold over the region has rarely been more evident.

REALITIES OF APARTHEID

HEALTH CARE
UNDER APARTHEID

Pippa Gordon

Rosa Chokoe climbed aboard a bus in her village and traveled 20 miles to the closest doctor because she was worried about pelvic pains. She was rewarded for her trouble and her $8 fee by being told she was "dirty inside."

Rosa left the white doctor's office with a pack of pills and no explanation. The pains continued, and she returned twice, only to suffer the same indignities.

Like most women in South Africa's impoverished black tribal reservations, or "homelands," Rosa was in poor health. She made a bare living for herself and her three children by hawking fruits and vegetables. But Rosa was "an outstanding woman, very dedicated, sympathetic and energetic," in the words of Colette Caine of the nongovernmental Environmental and Development Agency. So the 400 women living in the Bochum area of Lebowa selected her as a community health organizer trainee.

It was an honor she had no opportunity to fulfill. After a sudden onset of vaginal bleeding and pelvic pain, she was rushed 70 miles to the nearest hospital, in the whites-only town of Pietersburg. There she was put on oxygen, given a blood transfusion, tested—and found to have advanced cervical cancer. Within a year, Rosa was dead at the age of 47.

Reprinted from Pippa Gordon, "Blacks' Health Neglected Under South African Apartheid," *Pacific News Service*, December 22, 1984.

Rosa's case is common in South Africa. Soweto, the black township of 1.5 million residents near Johannesburg, has the world's second-highest incidence of cervical cancer, according to Dr. Gladwyn Leiman of the South African Institute for Medical Research. What makes this grim statistic all the more shocking is that a simple, inexpensive annual exam can detect cervical cancer when it can still be treated.

Apartheid Health Care

This is a nation of extreme contrasts between black and white, rich and poor, and the health system is no exception. The stunning medical breakthrough represented by Dr. Christiaan Barnard's pioneering heart transplant operation stands in stark contrast to the woefully inadequate medical care available to the black majority.

These disparities are the inevitable outcome of the government's apartheid policies. Under apartheid, 4.5 million whites rule over 25 million disenfranchised blacks, and reserve the best of everything for themselves. In Kwa Zulu, one of the homelands, the budget for health services, including 26 hospitals, is roughly equivalent to the budget for Groote Schuur, the Cape Town hospital where Dr. Barnard practices.

In white Johannesburg, one doctor serves every 900 people. In Kwa Zulu, there is one doctor for every 17,500 people—and one for every 116,000 people in Qwa Qwa, another homeland.

Authorities here proudly point out that the infant mortality rate for whites is only 9 per 1,000 live births—below U.S. rates. But UNICEF reports South Africa as a whole has one of the world's highest infant mortality rates in relation to national wealth—as high as 282 per 1,000 in some parts of the country, meaning that more than a quarter of all babies born die during their first year.

These babies, like those in other underdeveloped countries, are killed by malnutrition and related diseases, as well as by gastroenteritis, measles, typhoid, cholera and polio. It is not unusual to find small mounds of earth topped with a baby's bottle or perhaps a toy in rural graveyards.

The cause of death is not so easy to find. In 1964, more than 13,000 blacks, mostly children, were reported to suffer from kwashiorkor—severe malnutrition—and only one white. But there is no way of comparing that with recent experience because the country has not kept count of kwashiorkor cases since 1964.

Black Health Ignored

This is the policy with many diseases common among blacks. In May, Dr. Nak van der Merwe, health and welfare minister, told the all-white parliament that keeping data on malnutrition was useless, as cases are hard to diagnose and the term itself "ill-defined."

Disease and hunger permeate the 10 arid "homelands"—only 13 percent of South Africa's land—where blacks are required to live unless they have a special pass. Yet homeland medical services are often poor. Mothers who get to baby clinics—a 20-mile walk for some—frequently receive cursory care. Inadequate refrigeration means vaccines become ineffective. During a recent polio epidemic in one homeland, Ganzakulu, investigators found polio vaccines which would not work at six clinics.

Overcrowding in the homelands makes even bare subsistence farming impossible, so the residents—mostly women, children, the aged—often depend completely on money sent by family members working in the white cities. According to a study sponsored by the Carnegie Foundation of New York, 81 percent of homeland residents live below a minimum economic level and 1.5 million have no income at all.

Because of the recent drought, an estimated 2.4 million people—about a quarter of all homeland residents—need emergency food aid.

The white government's response to all this has frequently been to threaten coercive population control. "Statistics show that we must dramatically cut the population growth, whether it is in the black man's nature to do it or not. Otherwise we are going to all die of thirst," Environment and Fisheries Minister Sarel Hayward recently warned.

The Government's 'Solution'

So government expenditures on family planning continue to rise while health budgets affecting millions—such as the tuberculosis program—are cut back. And, unlike most health services, family planning services are offered at no cost.

The most frequently used contraceptive method in the homelands is the controversial Depo-Provera, recently banned in the United States, which is easy to administer and lasts three to six months—but which has been associated with such side effects as heavy bleeding, headaches, loss of sexual drive, and prolonged temporary sterility. It can take as long as two years for a woman to conceive after coming off "the shot." But those who get the injection are not told of any of these side effects.

A few resilient organizations continue to work to improve the situation in the homelands, but they cannot stop the upward spiral of poverty and the ill health which accompanies it. University of Cape Town economist Francis Wilson, who headed the Carnegie study, believes a country rich in gold and diamonds can rectify this situation. "We have just completed a century of industrialization," he said. "We're exporting food while people are starving here. We have the means to put it right."

6 REALITIES OF APARTHEID

WOMEN UNDER APARTHEID

Margaret Mackay

The South African people have waged a long and determined struggle for liberation—and in that struggle, women have played a central role.

African National Congress President Oliver Tambo declared, "In our beleaguered country, the woman's place is in the battlefront of struggle," when he declared 1984 the "Year of the Woman" on behalf of the ANC.

Perhaps the fact that Black women are the most heavily oppressed by the apartheid system—on the basis of their race, their class, and their sex—explains why they have opposed it with such courage and determination. . . .

Special Oppression of Women

This system scars the life of every Black South African—but women bear the brunt of it.

Many South African women must struggle alone to support children and aged relatives on the barren reserves, apart from husbands and fathers who have sought work in the cities.

Others, driven by the need to earn a living, must leave their children behind and move illegally to the urban areas in search of work. An intricate series of laws prevents them from settling in the cities. Most women are faced daily with the possibility of being "repatriated" to the area where they were born, or to a "homeland" they have never seen, or removed to resettlement camps.

Reprinted from Margaret Mackay, South African Women on the Battlefront for Liberation," *Daily World*, March 7, 1985, p. 12M.

It is almost impossible for a husband and wife to secure the legal right to live together in an urban area. This is why squatter camps—where Black families live together illegally, risking raids, arrests, and fines—have grown up on the outskirts of many townships, like the famous Crossroads camp outside Cape Town. The apartheid government has been trying to bulldoze the camp since 1977, but the women have courageously and successfully resisted this. This February, at least 18 people were killed and scores were wounded in new government efforts to destroy Crossroads.

Black Women as Workers

Black women today make up one-third of the African labor force. Most are limited to low paid, unskilled or semi-skilled work. Even when they do the same work as men, they are discriminated against in pay and working conditions. The average earnings of African women are less than half those of African men, and in 1980 they earned only 8% of the income of white men.

Most Black women work as domestic workers. They receive low wages for unrestricted hours of isolated work, caring for the children of white families while their own children are left behind on the reserves.

Agricultural workers are even more exploited. With the increasing mechanization of South African agriculture, many have been forced off the farms they lived and worked on for decades. Most have become seasonal workers.

They are often paid in kind, rather than cash. Their wages are even lower than those of domestic workers and, like them, they are not covered by minimum wage, unemployment benefits or other forms of social security.

A very small proportion of African women work in industry—concentrated in the clothing, textile, food processing and canning plants, where women's wages are significantly lower than those of men.

Only a handful of women are employed as technicians or professionals, mostly as teachers and nurses. By the mid-1970's, there still was not one African woman lawyer, magistrate, engineer, architect, veterinarian, chemist or pharmacist.

High unemployment has affected Black men and women in all types of work since the early 1970's.

Source:

CALC Report, April, 1985

Women in the Struggle

"The women are the most oppressed of the Black majority, and perhaps that explains why women have been so much in the forefront of the liberation struggle," says Nomazizi Sokudela, a member of the Women's Section of the ANC. "It also explains why we have seen the struggle for equality, for women's rights, as an integral part of the national liberation struggle.

"Women's inequality has been imposed by the regime—for example, in laws which make women perpetual minors, unable to engage in contracts, to own or dispose of property, or even to serve as legal guardians of our own children."

One leader in South Africa's liberation struggle was Charlotte Maxeke, a founding member of the ANC, who played an important role in the struggle against the 1913 Land Act and helped found the ANC Women's League in 1913.

In the same period, women resisted government efforts to make them carry passes. Their resistance was so successful that the idea was not raised again until the mid-1950s. . . .

The Anti-pass Struggles

Women also led the massive anti-pass campaigns that erupted across South Africa in the mid-'50s. A UN publication describes some of these courageous actions: "On 9 August 1956, in a protest organized by FSAW (Federation of South African Women), more than 20,000 women came to the Union Buildings in Pretoria to see the Prime Minister. When he refused to see them, they placed petitions with more than 100,000 signatures in his office. . . .

"On the day that passes were to be distributed in Sanderton in southeastern Transvaal, all 914 women who went to protest to the Mayor were arrested for taking part in an illegal procession.

"But the women were undaunted. In July 1957, in Gopane Village in the Baphurutse reserve, some women burned their passes. When 35 women were arrested, 233 more volunteered to be arrested. . . .In June 1957, at Pietersburg in the northern Transvaal, 2,000 women stoned officials who came to register them. . . .In October 1957, in Johannesburg, more than 2,000 were arrested" protesting government efforts to register them.

In the same period, women organized a bus boycott in the Black townships of Alexandra, Sophiatown and Lady Shelburne to protest a fare increase. In mass raids, 6,606 Africans were arrested, and another 7,860 were subpoenaed. But the Africans continued to protest, and after five months the fare increase was rolled back.

Women in the Underground

A wave of repression swept South Africa after the Sharpeville massacre in 1960. Nomazizi Sokudela points out that many women were arrested and imprisoned or banished.

"When the movement went underground, a lot of women left the country to work in the various structures of the movement in exile, whilst others remained and have worked actively in the underground structures inside the country," she said.

"They have also participated fully in the military wing of the ANC, Umkhonto we Sizwe. Thandi Modise, who was arrested in action, is serving an eight-year sentence in South Africa now.

"Dorothy Nyembe, who finished a 15-year prison term in March 1984, has been outstanding in her courageous participation in the liberation struggle. . .and Lillian Keagile. Now these are women who, on top of being imprisoned, are subjected also to torture and rape.". . .

Nomzamo Winnie Mandela has spent almost all of her adult life under banning orders, in prison, or in banishment, with only one 12-month period of freedom since 1963, and has only enjoyed two years of married life with her husband since their marriage in 1958. Nelson Mandela went underground after the ANC was banned in 1960, was arrested a year later and has been serving a life sentence ever since.

In 1977, she was banished to a "living grave" outside the remote township of Brandfort. Repeated government efforts to convict and imprison her have ended in failure—and brought international attention to her plight.

Winnie Mandela has refused to allow her incarceration in Brandfort to break her spirit, or to undermine her confidence that the future belongs to the South African people.

The women of South Africa continue their struggle in the same determined spirit—by defending the squatter camps, defying mass removals, supporting their children's struggle against "Bantu education."

7 REALITIES OF APARTHEID

CHILDREN UNDER APARTHEID

International Defence and Aid Fund for Southern Africa

The main victims of the apartheid system of racial domination in South Africa are children—the children of the oppressed black majority.

Racial discrimination is the basis of the apartheid system. In South Africa every child is classified at birth according to the colour of his or her skin. This racial classification controls each individual's life from the cradle to the grave: a child's colour determines its whole future.

The mortality rate for African infants is six times higher than the white rate, because of poverty and inadequate health care. For those that survive there is a divisive school system which not only denies black children access to equal educational opportunities but aims to prepare them to serve white society.

Deprivation and neglect extend to leisure opportunities. White children enjoy outstanding sports and recreational facilities, which are not available to black children. The poverty of their parents often obliges black children to contribute to the family income. The exploitation of child labor is widespread in South Africa both on the farms and in the cities.

Even the basic right of a child to family life is undermined by the system of migrant labor which is the basis of the apartheid economy. Many African children are prevented by law from living with parents working in 'white' areas, but white children suffer no similar disadvantage.

Excerpt taken from *Children Under Apartheid,* published by the International Defence and Aid Fund for Southern Africa, London, 1980.

All residential areas are segregated and housing conditions for black families are generally poor and inferior to white conditions. Black children live in overcrowded homes lacking in amenities such as electricity and indoor sanitation. Many live in shacks in 'squatter' settlements; others are literally homeless, sleeping rough and scavenging for food.

Most white children enjoy security and the normal benefits of citizenship. African children, on the other hand, may be subject to forced removal with their families to barren rural areas in the Bantustans, designated as 'Black Homelands'. Under the Bantustan program they are also being deprived of South African citizenship and made aliens in the land of their birth.

Child Labor

When white children leave school, having received a good, free education, they can hope to obtain well-paid employment. Many go on to further training. A black child, poorly educated, and often needing to help with family finances, cannot expect to find a fulfilling and well-paid job. Moreover, the use of black children as underpaid and exploited workers is widespread.

Although it is illegal in South Africa to employ any child under the age of 16, many black children are obliged to work in order to survive. With disintegration of many family units because of the migrant labor system, some black children are homeless and have to find some means of supporting themselves. In the farming areas, black children are expected to work alongside their parents, for pitiful wages or food rations.

In the urban areas, there are many instances of illegal employment of child labor. One report describes children aged 10-15 from the black areas around Johannesburg roaming the streets in search of work as kitchen cleaners, shop workers, domestic servants and street vendors. They are rarely paid more than R6 for a six-day week; sometimes food is included as a form of payment. Many of these children sleep on their employers' premises in storerooms and on kitchen floors. They do not go to school, and many suffer from illnesses associated with poverty and malnutrition. There is often no escape from this life of toil; employers warn the children that they will be arrested if they try to run away.

Children are also employed, illegally, in factories and workshops, in menial, badly-paid jobs. In 1978 *Post* newspaper, investigating child labor, reported that boys aged 9-11 were working in shops and market stalls in Johannesburg. Their employers told the reporter that the boys pestered them for work, in order to contribute to the family income. . . .

Housing and Homelessness

The largest black township in South Africa is Soweto, which has an estimated population of over one million. Its inhabitants serve the industrial and commercial needs of Johannesburg, but they must live in a segregated ghetto.

Township houses are small and bare. Typically they consist of four rooms only. In Soweto houses are occupied by between seven and 14 persons. Only 25% of the houses have inside running water, 15% have electricity, 7% a bath or shower and 3% hot water.

The township environment is bleak. There are few large buildings, except police stations, administrative blocks, migrant workers' hostels and beer halls. The rest of the dwellings are single-story houses, row upon row, divided by pitted roads and interspersed with old mine dumps and waste ground. The roads are dusty in winter and muddy in summer. Few areas have street lighting and there are not many public telephones or other facilities. Buses and trains run in the mornings and evenings to take black workers to their jobs, but otherwise the townships are geographically isolated from the cities and towns their residents serve. . . .

Black children thus tend to live in very overcrowded conditions. There is a chronic shortage of housing throughout the black community. Most places have endless waiting lists; several families often share a small house, living in one room each; every household accommodates relatives and lodgers who cannot find anywhere else to stay. . . .

Squatter settlements also exist in the Bantustan areas. Winterveld, in the BophuthaTswana Bantustan near Pretoria, is one example. Originally intended as a temporary home for Africans removed from white farms and urban townships, it has grown into a huge rambling complex of shacks, without water supplies or sanitation. The inhabitants look for work in the industrial areas around Pretoria. Because many of them are there without permits their homes have been raided and the people threatened with eviction even though they have nowhere else to go. The authorities have threatened to cut off old age and disability pensions, and to demolish schools which the community has itself built. Families and children experience acute insecurity, not knowing when they will be forced to move, or where they will go.

Life is hardly less secure in the official townships, particularly for wives and children, who possess few rights. Tenancy of township houses is given only to men in the first instance. Wives and children may be evicted if the husband dies, or there is a divorce. If a man fails to pay his rent, he and his family are evicted and no alternative housing is provided. Some families shelter where they can, in abandoned vehicles and derelict buildings. Those without means of support, which often means women and small children, can be sent to transit camps, to await deportation to a Bantustan.

In this constant shifting and eviction of individuals and groups, to maintain the apartheid aim of racial separation, many black families are unavoidably split up. Children are separated from their parents and learn to be self-reliant at an early age.

Homeless children find they can scavenge and earn a meager living in the cities, if they keep out of the way of the authorities. They sleep rough, on their own or in pitiful little groups, and have no-one to care for them. Such are the victims of apartheid.

8   REALITIES OF APARTHEID

THE TORTURE AND TERROR: ENFORCING APARTHEID

Gay J. McDougall

Allegations of maltreatment and torture of political detainees have become commonplace in South Africa. The allegations, made by defendants, state witnesses, and detainees, have been detailed and consistent. The pattern that emerges, on examining these allegations and the physical evidence of brutality, is that torture is routinely used by the security police during interrogations.

Various methods of torture have been described: electric shocks to the body, being made to assume a sitting position without the support of a chair—"the invisible chair," wearing shoes containing small stones for long periods of time, driving nails through the genitals of males, deprivation of sleep, food and toilet facilities, prolonged interrogation, psychological disorientation through long-term solitary confinement, hooding and suffocating, choking, arduous physical exercise and common assault such as slapping, kicking, beating with hosepipes and sticks, crushing of toes and banging detainees' heads on walls and tables. Several international organizations such as Amnesty International, United Nations Center Against Apartheid, the Ad Hoc Working Group of Experts of the United Nations Commission on Human Rights and International Defence and Aid Fund for Southern Africa have heard and documented sworn statements from ex-detainees and prisoners. . . .

Reprinted from "Deaths in Detention and South Africa's Security Laws," Lawyers' Committee for Civil Rights Under Law (Washington, September, 1983) pp. 5-12.

Important evidence of torture emerged from the recent inquest into the death of Neil Aggett. On 5 Feb. 1982, Dr. Aggett, secretary of the African Food and Cannery Workers Union, died in detention at John Vorster Square in Johannesburg, marking the first such death of a white political prisoner. Aggett was detained on 27 Nov. 1981 under the Internal Security Act in a wave of detentions of trade unionists. Two weeks later he was moved to Johannesburg from Pretoria Central Prison after it was ordered that he be detained under Section 6 of the Terrorism Act. It appears that except during times of interrogation, Aggett was kept in solitary confinement, and it was on 5 February that police reported they found Aggett hanging in his cell.

On the day before Aggett's death, he made a written complaint about his treatment to a security police sergeant. He alleged that he was beaten by police, left bleeding, blindfolded with a towel, and subjected to electric shock through handcuffs. He was interrogated once for 62 hours non-stop and had spent 110 of the final 168 hours of his life in interrogation rooms. . . .

Premanathan Naidoo was under detention for questioning in John Vorster Square concurrently with Aggett. He testified during the Aggett inquest to having received torture from security police.

In a sworn affidavit, another detainee stated: "I was then handcuffed after they had padded my wrists and blindfolded me. I had to sit with my hands around my knees. A stick of some sort was then pushed between my arms and the back of my knees. They picked me up by the stick, and placed the stick on something so that I was hanging upside down. They told me that I was hanging outside the window. I then screamed because the handcuffs were biting into my shins. I was beaten about the face. . .to stop me screaming and, in the process, he broke his watch (its alarm went off). I am not sure whether I lost consciousness so I can't say how long I was hanging in this way. Eventually I was taken down and had lost all feeling in my legs. I had an injury to the back of my ankle which resulted from the leg iron."

Additional testimony at the inquest included an account of a torture method reportedly used by the South African security police that brings its victims seconds away from death by strangulation by means of a wet towel wrapped

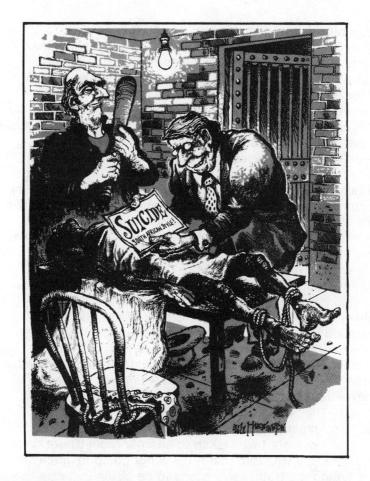

around the throat and pulled tight until the victim is about to faint. This method leaves no mark on the throat. If the interrogator miscalculates and the prisoner dies, the victim is said to be strung up in his cell—and the official explanation is that he has "committed suicide by hanging.". . .

The Record in Namibia

Details of torture, maltreatment, and physical violence during interrogation also have been vividly described by many Namibians in sworn testimonies to various international commissions. Axel Johannes, formerly SWAPO's (Southwest Africa People's Organization) Administrative Secretary inside Namibia, described his interrogation during a 1979 arrest by the South African security forces:

"During my detention I was subjected to many kinds of torture. On several occasions I was beaten with butts of rifles and pistols. I was handcuffed or chained around my ankles and then hung up with the tips of my feet just touching the floor. I was stripped naked and then beaten up with both a hose pipe and the handle of a pick-axe, to a state where I lost consciousness or even felt I was experiencing death. When I was bleeding, I was forced to lick up the blood from the floor. I was even buried alive in a river bed. On two separate occasions, they attempted to suffocate me by completely covering me with a blanket, putting me in the boot of a car and driving me around for quite a long time. Electric shocks were administered to my male organs. I was prevented from sleeping for 14 days, day and night. Sometimes I had to go up to five days without food."

Rauna Nambinga, a Namibian nurse and SWAPO member, testified before the Second Session of the International Commission of Inquiry into the Crimes of the Racist and Apartheid Regimes in Southern Africa during 1981 about her torture at the hands of the South African security police, including electric shock and beatings: "[T]he day I remember as the the most terrible was when I was taken to a small room [where] there were many pictures of dead people on the wall. They told me one of those people was my brother, . . .so I must show them which one was likely to be his. . . .From there I was taken to another room where there were snakes. I was told that if I was not going to agree and start telling the truth, I was going to be bitten by those snakes. . .one man. . .fetched one snake and came with it towards me. . .then the man with the snake came. . .and placed the head of the snake on my left ear. Then I felt pain which I could not tell exactly, whether it was the snake biting me then, or some instrument used on my body. . .I spent more than four hours in that snake room. . . ."

Redress from the Courts

On only two occasions have security police officers been charged with culpability in the death of political detainees. Neither case resulted in a conviction despite the finding by the presiding magistrate for the inquest into the death of

Isaac Muofhe that Muofhe's death had been caused by police assault during interrogation. The two policemen who were subsequently charged with Muofhe's murder were acquitted after the court ruled that the transcript of the inquest containing incriminating statements made by the policemen was inadmissible evidence at their trial.

On several occasions, civil actions for damages arising from the deaths of political detainees have been brought against the South African government. Rather than face a full investigation into police interrogation methods, the government has often chosen to settle these claims out of court.

CASE STUDY ON TORTURE: A TALE OF HOPE AND DESPAIR[1]

Ndanganeni Phaswana's tormentors told him he had been cursed the day he was born, and for four months they gave him every reason to believe it.

No, said the Lutheran pastor from South Africa, he rarely felt holy throughout his nightmare of nearly three years ago—a nightmare which, he said, may not have ended. And no, said St. Olaf College's first visiting pastor, he rarely felt human throughout his ordeal.

But between the beatings which left him a "disfigured skeleton," the seemingly endless electric shocks to his ears and genitals, and the tearing out of his pubic and facial hair, Phaswana said he always found time to pray.

"I prayed for them to kill me," he said from his office in St. Olaf's Boe Memorial Chapel.

These days, the 34-year-old pastor says he has rarely felt so full of life. The St. Olaf community has adopted as well as accepted him.

The faculty and students raised more than $3,500 to have Phaswana's wife and three young children flown 9,000 miles from South Africa to Minnesota. They were to arrive last night and will stay in Minnesota for four weeks.

1 Reprinted from Paul Levy, "South African Pastor Tells of Hope and Despair," Minneapolis Star and Tribune, December 23, 1984.

"What the school has done means more to me than I can express," Phaswana said, "In return, I hope to share my story and hope people here can learn something from it. That will be my Christmas gift to Minnesota."

Here is Phaswana's story:

South Africa has been a land of apartheid and turmoil for years, one in which many blacks and whites have dedicated their lives to killing one another. Bombings are not uncommon.

In October 1981, the Sibasa police station was bombed. A group quickly claimed responsibility for the bombing in a confession broadcast by the British Broadcasting Company.

The confession seemed to matter little to the local secret police, who stopped Phaswana two blocks from his house on Jan. 5, 1982.

"They accused me of the bombing and said I was cursed the day I was born," said Phaswana. "That evening, at the detention center, they gave me pen and paper to write a confession."

Phaswana said he wrote a sermon instead.

The next morning, he reiterated his innocence to security police but to no avail. He was taken to an office where police yanked hair from several parts of his body and then made him stand upside down against a wall.

"I didn't believe that could happen to a human being." he said.

But the torture he had endured was nothing compared to what happened next.

The guards continued to ask Phaswana to confess to the bombing and tell where he had hidden an arsenal of weapons. He pleaded his innocence.

"They made me take off my clothes and they handcuffed my hands behind my back," Phaswana said. "They put electrodes on my earlobes and covered me with a canvas bag. Then they poured liquid over me.

"They would ask me questions and when I told the truth and did not say what they wanted to hear, the electric shocks were flipped on. They did this on and off for several hours.

"The electrodes were touching my shoulders and every time they flipped on the switch, the pain was so great that I believed my neck was out of my body. But I was still alive,

My Worst Detention

The third and last of my detentions was the worst. Twenty people were arrested on November 18, 1981, shortly after the bombing of several police stations. I had absolutely nothing to do with the bombing and they knew it, but it was a golden opportunity for discipline. They tortured us brutally. In the first day one man died from the abuse. They banged my head against the wall, beat me up, kicked my private parts. They used sticks and chains to hit me. They applied electric shock. Two weeks after the shock I suffered a heart attack. A week later a second. After a third heart attack, they hospitalized me on February 19, 1982. My ear drums had been perforated. I had wounds on my knees and my whole body was swollen from the torture. After 106 days in the hospital, I was released on June 1, 1982. I was later hospitalized for further treatment and most recently had an operation last March on my vocal cords. It is a miracle that I am now generally fine except for slight pains.

Two other pastors and myself brought a civil damages claim against the government for the torture we suffered in incommunicado detention. The suit was settled out of court March 5, 1984.

Reverend Dean T. Simon Farisani, *House Foreign Affairs Committee*, June 21, 1984

so I knew that wasn't so.

"I wanted to be dead."

"Then it got worse."

Phaswana said the electrodes were connected to his navel. Then, his genitals. Electric shocks were sent through his body for several hours. With each shock, he bit his lip or tongue until they were puffed and bloody.

The pain was excruciating. He fabricated a story. Something about guns being hidden in a mountain cave in a place he had never been. The covering and handcuffs were removed. He was to lead his tormentors to the hidden weapons.

"About half way, I told them I was lying because of the pain and I wanted them to kill me," Phaswana said.

He was returned to the detention center, where he received more shocks and a beating. His right eye was punched closed. Today, his small finger on his right hand is noticeably deformed—the result of guards stepping on his hands.

The torture continued, on and off, the next six days. On Jan. 12, he again received a shock to his genitals.

"But this one was different," he said. "It was so powerful that my diaphragm made a deep sound which was like the bellowing of a bull. Then, they stopped. It was awful, so awful that not even my persecutors could stand it."

After being beaten the next day, Phaswana was told he had been labeled a communist and would be sentenced to death. While sitting in solitary confinement, he prayed for death.

"When it didn't happen, I began to doubt God's existence," he said. "I put my arms against the wall and leaned forward. I felt a heavy pain and quickly asked God's forgiveness.

"That's when I saw Christ standing before me, showing his own scars. His were like mine. The mere presence of Christ in that cell made me happy. I thought, 'If God and I are both communists, who am I to grumble?' "

A few days later, Phaswana was charged with two counts of murder and three counts of attempted murder. He asked God if he would be convicted.

"I heard a voice," Phaswana said. "He told me, 'Don't worry. It will be a matter of days.' "

On Feb. 12, a magistrate was told of Phaswana's torture. Phaswana showed his scars. The judge was stunned. Word of Phaswana's beatings quickly spread to several human rights organizations—including Amnesty International and the British Council of Churches.

The state dropped all charges against Phaswana on May 28, 1982. No explanation was given. None was requested.

Phaswana was able to return to his parish in the Angelico Lutheran Church of South Africa. When the American Lutheran Church and his church agreed to begin an exchange program, Phaswana was chosen to go to America. He received a letter from St. Olaf Pastor Benson last May and arrived in Northfield by summer's end.

At St. Olaf College, Phaswana consults with students and leads chapel services Sundays and Wednesday nights. Much of his time is spent visiting area churches, where he has told his story to others, Benson said.

This summer, he will return to South Africa, where, he said, he may be punished for telling his tale. Yet, it is a story that must be told, he said.

Benson said: "There's so much to be learned from his story—about his relationship with God, about apartheid, about African issues."

"You know, I remember him saying he thought it a miracle that he could look at a white face and smile. I'm thankful for that miracle."

CHAPTER 2

INTERNAL RESISTANCE AND
POLITICAL CHANGE

THE INTERNAL RESISTANCE

APARTHEID IS CHANGING

The South African Government

*The following comments are excerpted from a public state-
ment on racial progress in South Africa by the South African
Department of Foreign Affairs.*

Points to Consider

1. Why do South African cities attract black workers?
2. Where do these workers come from?
3. Why has racial discrimination almost disappeared?
4. What has happened to black wages?

Excerpted from a South African Government public position statement on black economic and social progress in *South Africa*,
January, 1985.

A survey by a firm of management consultants embracing 167 large South African companies revealed that seven out of 10 firms disregard race for promotion.

It is common knowledge that South African metropolitan areas are such an irresistible magnet for Black workers from all parts of the African subcontinent that strict influx control measures—now being humanized to let in people with work and accommodation—have been applied, and the economies of neighboring countries such as Lesotho, Mozambique and Transkei depend to a considerable extent on migrant workers in South African mines.

A typical lunch-hour scene at a Pretoria supermarket illustrates the fruits plucked by Black urban workers. A dozen mainly Black cashiers sell trolley-loads of groceries and other household goods to lines of sophisticated urbanites, at least half of whom are black.

On Saturday mornings the shopping centres of small towns throughout the country are usually dominated mainly by Black shoppers.

Living Standards

This is in stark contrast to the position on South Africa's eastern fringes where, at the height of the recent drought, hundreds of people a day would slip illegally across the border seeking work on farms "just for bread, not money."

Fortunately, the World Bank is to step up aid to famine-ridden regions of Southern Africa. The Development Bank of Southern Africa and the South African Department of Foreign Affairs undertake similar co-operative development projects with some of its Black independent neighbors.

While urban Black South African living standards have long been the envy of the African subcontinent, it is the Government's acceptance, in the early 1980's, of all the major recommendations of the enlightened Wiehahn and Riekert reports that have really opened the door to Black advancement in every field of endeavor to the highest level of achievement.

In shops, banks, building societies and other private firms, people of all races are being trained as cashiers, clerks, foremen and the like, often in special colleges established by the firms.

Source: *South African Panorama*

Today, anyone who wants to work, irrespective of race, creed or sex, has the right and the opportunity to develop into a useful citizen, since the country's progress and prosperity depends on the continual improvement of its people's quality of life.

Racial Discrimination

Institutionalized (State-enforced) racial discrimination has today almost totally disappeared from the South African labor scene.

One of the first steps was to repeal all job reservation, which means that virtually all careers everywhere in the country are open to all people on a merit basis.

Blacks qualifying for permanent residence in the big cities are absolved from registering as workseekers, and can also move to other cities if they change their jobs.

They can practice any type of business in their residential areas which means, for example, that Soweto is changing Johannesburg's 'dormitory' city to an economic entity with a developing Central Business District and scores of small Black industries.

Racial Discrimination

A survey by a firm of management consultants embracing 167 large South African companies revealed that seven out of 10 firms disregard race for promotion, more than half have employees of all population groups working together at the same level, and more than six in ten have integrated pay structures for all workers, i.e. paying the rate for the job. Eight in ten have racially mixed offices, and nearly seven in ten think it possible to eliminate all discrimination within five years.

Apart from America's Sullivan principles, European Economic Community firms also have a code of employment practice, as well as South African firms.

There are frequent seminars for Black businessmen, with Businessmen-of-the-Year functions. The Black consumer market is rocketing, the wage gap is narrowing, particularly in fields like mining and teaching, and in many big firms. Fringe benefits are being substantially improved. The Government has passed legislation obliging employers to improve the safety, security and health of their workers, and provide for unemployment insurance, accident cover and medical plans.

A survey indicates that separate pension plans for women and Blacks are being phased-out.

Real Black wages in the non-agricultural sector rocketed by 78.5 per cent between 1972 and 1983. A survey reveals that by the year 2000 the local Black market will be twice the size of the total current consumer market in South Africa. A commercial bank estimates that, by 1985, Blacks will account for nearly half the private consumer spending. The new South African labor legislation is more enlightened than in most countries today, even including the Western World, promoting as it does the highest degree of worker peace, training and protection. It is, indeed, something to be proud of; a beacon of hope for the entire African subcontinent.

As an important link between employer and employee, all workers may form or join trade unions of their choice. There is various machinery, including negotiation, arbitration and industrial courts, for settling labor disputes.

A National Manpower Commission advises the Government on matters of labor policy and law. Its role is strongly backed by research on a national and international level.

Mainstay for Region

In many respects South Africa is the mainstay of the entire region. Services and assistance provided by South Africa are often the most important stabilizing factor in the subcontinent.

South African Government, September, 1985

The Commission has appointed standing committees on employment creation, labor relations, education and training, conditions of employment, social security, employment services, productivity and international labor affairs.

The Manpower Training Act has eliminated all distinctions of race and sex in its efforts to co-ordinate training services.

A National Training Board has been established to which all employers pay a compulsory levy. Eight Government industrial training centres, suitably equipped by the private sector, offer in-service training in all cities. In 1982, 405,000 mainly Black people were trained in 198 group and 887 private training centres.

Tax rebates for factory training courses are usually worth more than the cost of the training.

The State trains early school-leavers free of charge at group training centres, and offers vocational counselling and placement services to match the person to the job at all educational levels.

The crying need for skilled workers means that Blacks from universities and matriculation classes are readily accommodated by the public and private sector as personnel officers, accountants, salesmen, artisans, teachers and nurses—the list is legion.

The Government aims at producing a substantial core of contented businessmen, property owners, and well-paid workers in all communities on the principle that the economic cake must be seen to be available to all on merit.

All national servicemen are entitled to free apprenticeship training, and since the beginning of the decade Black apprentices have also been tested at the huge Olifantsfontein testing centre. The number of Black apprentices in the engineering, automotive and building industries is mushrooming apace, and qualified Black, Coloured and Indian artisans are employed in hundreds of factories and businesses throughout the country.

The Government is committed to upgrading the quality of life of Black communities.

As regards housing and community development, it establishes infrastructures such as water, electricity and roads for the private sector to build on, and has made available all its rented houses for sale to the public of all race groups.

In Soweto, the large Black city on the outskirts of Johannesburg, at least 60 Black building firms are operating, as well as several estate agencies and scores of cement-brickmaking firms and private draughtsmen to design new and extended homes for a veritable building boom sparked off by the 99-year leasehold project, which amounts to home ownership.

The homes are financed by building societies and other financial institutions, as well as by local development boards.

10 THE INTERNAL RESISTANCE

GROWING REPRESSION
AND RESISTANCE

Jennifer Davis

Jennifer Davis is an Executive Director of the American Committee on Africa. The following article was excerpted from her article in the CALC Report, the national journal of the Clergy and Laity Concerned, an action-oriented interfaith peace and justice organization.

Points to Consider

1. What are the sources of black resistance?
2. How are whites involved in the resistance?
3. What is AZAPO? What are the UDF and the ANC?
4. How is the new constitution described?

Jennifer Davis, "Growing Resistance and Repression in South Africa," *CALC Report,* April, 1985.

*The Black majority population is still totally ex-
cluded from participation in South African society,
except as cheap laborers.*

Black resistance to white minority rule is as old as the
first act of colonial conquest in South Africa. During the past
ten years, however, the confrontation has grown harsher as
black forces drew strength from the victories won by armed
struggle in Angola, Mozambique, and Zimbabwe.

Throughout the 1970s, pressure on the system was
generated by the increasing militancy and organizational
sophistication of the black population.

Early in the decade, workers, first in Namibia and then all
across South Africa, began to challenge the terrible conditions under which they worked. Higher wages were only a
small part of their demands; other demands included the
right to unionize, the right to strike, and the right to work
freely.

By 1976 the new wave of militancy had swept up the student population: some 1,000 students were killed as they
protested in the hundreds of thousands against apartheid-
style education and a future as perpetual second-class
visitors in the land of their birth.

The state's immediate response was to shoot, but in the
back-rooms, the planners of apartheid moved rapidly to
design what they hoped would be a more adaptable form of
apartheid. By 1983 they had produced a new constitution
whose aim was to draw in some sections of the Black
population with the promise of limited access to power. In
reality these reforms were tainted by apartheid forms. They
allowed a vote and role in Parliament to two ethnically identified sections of the Blacks, the "coloreds" and people of
Indian origin, but only in a strictly segregated manner. Thus
South Africa now has three Houses of Parliament, one for
each ethnic group, except the majority population, the more
than 22 million Africans.

The Black majority population is still totally excluded from
participation in South African society, except as cheap
laborers. These are people with no rights: no right to vote,

no right to live together as man and wife (even if legally married), no right to live where they please, or to seek work freely in the cities where jobs may be had, and no right to own land or citizenship in South Africa.

Source:
CALC Report, April, 1985

Many Forms of Struggle

While almost all of South Africa's black population (except the few in government pay) would celebrate the end of apartheid, that population is far from homogeneous in terms of its group and class interests, or its political alignments.

There are deep divisions over such issues as collaboration on any level with government institutions such as local councils, the new parliamentary system, or bantustan administration. Rejection of a leadership role for democratic whites in the liberation struggle distinguishes "black consciousness" organizations from those which argue for some form of multiracialism or non-racialism. There are also political differences within each of these two political groupings. Some so-called "black consciousness" organizations, such as the Azanian People's Organization (AZAPO) which protested the recent Kennedy visit to South Africa, have sought to develop a socialist analysis; others, sometimes referred to as the nationalists, define themselves politically primarily in terms of color. Generally the various groups which reject a white leadership role tend to be linked in a loose alliance known as the National Forum. Those who argue for a multiracial or non-racial form of organization are currently united under the umbrella of the United Democratic Front which now encompasses over 700 organizations.

There are also profound differences between sectors of the black body politic who urge the need for working class leadership and supporters of more middle-class forms of organization.

Finally the commitment to some form of armed struggle separates the more radical stream from respected, reformist anti-apartheid leaders such as Bishop Desmond Tutu and the Rev. Allan Boesak.

Student protests and school boycotts involved as many as a million young people as tensions built during 1984. Student rejection of apartheid has ebbed and flowed in the eight years since the June 1976 Soweto student rebellion, but student militancy has never totally disappeared.

There are an estimated 5 million black youths in schools; many of them begin school much later than U.S. students or South African whites, so that black teenagers are often in primary school while black high school students are frequently young adults. In a recent move which students interpret as being aimed at activists, authorities have introduced upper age limits, so that a twenty year old may be refused entry into the last two years of high school. Only a few thousand black students manage to graduate from high school each year, and more than 80 percent never get beyond the primary grades. Schools are overcrowded, staffed by untrained personnel, and run with draconian regulations.

Fighting Phony Reforms

Under the new constitution there were to be 178 white members of a House of Assembly, 85 Colored members of a House of Representatives and 45 Indian members of a House of Delegates. It takes no mathematical genius to recognize that with such an arrangement the whites would remain in control.

In 1983, a storm of protest led to the formation of the

3.5 Million Removed

Sinte and her neighbors constituted what South African authorities call a "black spot," a concentration of blacks in areas reserved for whites or people of mixed race.

The soldiers threw Sinte's belongings onto a government truck and transported her 100 miles to an over-crowded, dust-choked "resettlement" village she had never known: Botshabelo.

On that day, Sinte became one of an estimated 3.5 million black South Africans forcibly moved out of "white areas" and into resettlement areas.

Minneapolis Tribune, September 8, 1985

United Democratic Front (UDF) which took on the task of mobilizing and uniting opposition. As its name suggests, the UDF is "a front made up of many different organizations, with different approaches to the problems that confront them, but with a willingness to come together on common issues." The national UDF is composed of community-based, single-focus organizations, many of which had been produced by local struggles. Thus in Natal, early members of the UDF included the Durban Housing Action Committee, the Joint Rent Committee and the Joint Commuters Committee. By mid-1984 the UDF had more than 600 affiliates. Its membership is open to black and white, and some of its leadership was closely associated with the now banned but still powerful African National Congress (ANC). Some progressive black organizations chose to oppose the new constitution from outside the UDF, but all were united in condemning and opposing this attempt to divide and rule.

The trade unions also displayed strong opposition to the new constitution while continuing to mobilize and organize on factory floor issues.

Role of Black Unions

Since 1979, when Africans were legally recognized as "employees" for the first time, Black unionism has been exploding, growing five times faster than that of whites. By 1983, black union membership had passed the 300,000 mark and new unions were being organized in key sectors such as the gold mines. Black workers make up over 80% of South Africa's work force, thus strong independent union organization poses a serious threat to the apartheid system . . .

Despite the differences among the trade unions, there is also keen recognition of the link between economic and political issues, and all the unions were engaged in opposing the new constitution. By the year's end, a major political strike—the Two-day Stay-away—had demonstrated the significant threat worker power poses to apartheid.

Armed Struggle

Formed more than seventy years ago, the African National Congress has continually been acknowledged as the major political organization representing Black aspirations, although its policies have been challenged by other political organizations such as the Pan Africanist Congress and the United Movement. Long dedicated to non-violent forms of passive resistance and civil disobedience, the Congress was driven by the apartheid regime's total intransigence to initiate limited forms of armed struggle in the 1960s.

In 1984, as mass-based popular action against apartheid was expanding, the underground network of the African National Congress demonstrated a growing capacity to sabotage targets in key areas. "Armed propaganda" is the term the ANC uses to describe the contemporary phase of its armed actions. Such actions are most often directed at economic and government targets such as power lines and stations, fuel depots, railway lines, police stations, or government offices. In 1983 a car-bomb explosion outside the headquarters of the South African Air Force, in which 19 people were killed, appeared to signal a new phase of more direct confrontation with the South African military forces.

An ANC speaker recently summarized the current balance of forces in South Africa. The South African regime is like a house owner beseiged by a cyclone, she said. When he closed the front door, the wind blew in the back. And when he shut the windows the roof blew off. And when he erected a temporary covering for the roof, the walls fell in.

11 THE INTERNAL RESISTANCE

I HAVE SEEN A LAND

Allan Boesak

Allan Boesak, president of the World Alliance of Reformed Churches, is chaplain at the University of the Western Cape in South Africa and a Sojourners *contributing editor. He is the leading advocate of non-violent resistance to apartheid.*

Points to Consider

1. Why was the Minister of Law and Order upset with Allan Boesak?
2. How is apartheid defined?
3. Why is it impossible to ban the United Democratic Front and other resistance movements in South Africa?
4. What kind of a land does Allan Boesak envision?

Allan Boesak, "A Reply to the Minister of Law and Order," *Sojourners,* February, 1985, pp. 28-30. Reprinted with permission of Sojourners, Box 29272, Washington, DC, 20017.

I have seen a land, not of apartheid, not of death, not of chains, but a land of joy and a land of freedom and a land of peace.

The Minister [of Law and Order, Louis Le Grange] has ordered that I be charged under Section 27 of the Police Act. . . .

Now, what angered the minister is apparently what I had said on a visit to Australia, where I had an interview with a person who had asked me what I thought about what is happening in South Africa. . . .

"What does it mean," he asked me, "when 7,000 troops are asked to go into, or ordered to go into, the [black] townships?" And I said that that means we have an undeclared state of civil war. I thought it was clear and honest, and I thought I was simply saying what I saw was the truth. The minister is upset about that.

He is even more upset because I talked about the role of the military and of the South African Defense Force. I said that we know they are committing unbelievable atrocities in the townships. . . .

A Violent System

Apartheid is a violent system. We have said so often before. It is a system that can only be maintained by ongoing violence, by wanton violence. It is a system that would not survive for one single moment if there were no police force, or if there were no army, or if there were no violent reaction from the government every single time the people protest.

In every police state, the police and the army are not really instruments at the service of all of the people, but they become instruments of the most vicious kind of oppression to maintain the position of power of those who see themselves as the powerful group. And this police state is no exception. This is what we have seen over the last three months. . . .

I have in my possession affidavits, and I will read simply a few examples of what has happened to people during the last few months since the police and the military invaded the townships, and since we have had this unrest. There was a little boy called Walter Pule Makhata, a schoolboy aged 14 from Naledi, Soweto. He went to the shop to buy a loaf of bread, was hit by birdshot, and found dead.

In Katlehong, three children, one of them mentally retarded, were allegedly assaulted by police on the 13th of September 1984. The police fired tear smoke into the house and walked in, asking where the children were. And when they found them, they started to kick and hit them all over their bodies. This happened to children. This is taken from a SACC affidavit. Who is the liar, Mr. Le Grange?

Source: *CALC Report*, April, 1985

On Friday, September 28, the horrendous example of the young boy who was shot in the police van by the policeman. His name is Jacob Moleleke.

On August 15 an unnamed boy, who called himself A.B., aged 15, was on the roof of his house in Watville Benoni, with two other people, doing repairs. There were no apparent disturbances in the area at that time. Then the police came through shooting tear gas cylinders. Some people ran out from the streets into A.B.'s house for shelter. The other two men on the roof fled, but he lay down on the roof. A policeman mounted the ladder to the roof, came up to him, and discharged a tear gas cylinder into his face. He has lost his left eye as a result.

If this is not an atrocity, what is? And if the minister does not know it, he must make it his business to know it.

Nicholas Mldulwa, 10 years old, was sent out by his father one evening to fetch firewood. The area was so quiet that his father actually thought that this was safe to do. A combi [station wagon] came by; a shot was fired. The father ran out and found his boy hit on the left side of his forehead with a rubber bullet. The police came and told him to keep the matter quiet. He refused, went to the lawyers, and signed an affidavit. He even gave the registration number of the vehicle.

Elsie Nana, 19 years old, was arrested while attending a prayer vigil. She was assaulted on the third of October, was told to write a statement and give details about whatever she knew about the activities of other people. She was two months pregnant. When she told them this during the assault, she was kicked and hit with a rubber baton repeatedly on her stomach.

All of this the minister can ask from the people who have made these affidavits. All I want to ask him is, "Who is the liar? Who is the slanderer? Who is the one who is trying to cover up deeds like this?"

Testify Against Evil

As long as these things happen, and as long as we hear about it, it will be our responsibility to testify against the evil that is gripping this country. We will not refuse. We will not stop doing this.

We will refuse to be intimidated. It seems to me that the

66

South African government thinks that these things that happen, these atrocities—yes, atrocities, Mr. Minister—will stop us from demanding our freedom. But the South African government must learn that the time that they can avert a change—a fundamental change in South Africa—by merely reaching for a gun is over. We will no longer be silenced by fear, or by intimidation, or even by the wanton killing of our people.

The demands are there and are clear: release the political prisoners; unban the organizations; scrap all these laws that have made South Africa a hell for so many people to live in; stop killing our children and our people on the street. Let us participate in an open, democratic society. Then there will be peace in this country.

The state threatens to ban the organizations, and they threaten to ban the United Democratic Front. It will be a little difficult because, I have often said, the UDF is the people of South Africa. They cannot ban the people. The UDF embodies the dreams of the people of South Africa, and they cannot ban that dream. The UDF embodies the aspiration of the people toward a free and just society. They cannot ban that. . . .

A New South Africa

I have seen a new South Africa. I have seen a land, not of apartheid, not of death, not of chains, but a land of joy and a land of freedom and a land of peace. Let us fight for that land. I have seen a new land where our children will no longer be bound down by the yoke of racism. Let us fight for that land. I have seen a land where our people shall work and enjoy the fruits of their labor. Let us fight for that land.

I have seen a land where families will no longer be broken up, and where mothers and fathers will enjoy the love and the respect of their children. Let us fight for that land. I have seen a land where the misery of relocation is no more, and where the graves dug for little children who will tomorrow die of hunger remain empty. Let us fight for that land.

I have seen a land where those of us who fight for freedom and for justice and for the self-respect of this country will no longer be sent to prison, will no longer be tortured, will no longer be threatened, will no longer be shot on the streets of our nation, but will be rewarded with honor and with the presence of justice. Let us fight for that land. And I have seen a land where we together will build something that is worthwhile, that is faithful to what we believe.

Let us not give that up, but make tonight a new dedication for that moment. Because I believe it does not matter what happens now. I believe that the freedom that we have struggled for and the freedom that we have died for will become a reality. You can make it happen. God bless you.

TRUE AGENTS OF PEACE

Desmond M. Tutu

Bishop Desmond Tutu is general secretary of the South African Council of Churches, the nation's main ecumenical body. The council represents 12 million South African churchgoers, of whom 88 per cent are black. Bishop Tutu won the Nobel Peace Prize.

Points to Consider

1. What is the attitude of the South African Government toward the South African Council of Churches?
2. How is the new constitution described?
3. What is happening in Namibia?
4. What is constructive engagement?

Excerpted from testimony before the House Foreign Affairs Sub-committee on Africa, December 4, 1984.

Apartheid is an evil as immoral and un-Christian in my view as Nazism, and in my view, the Reagan administration's support and collaboration with it is equally immoral, evil and totally un-Christian, without remainder.

The oppressed in South Africa and the lovers of freedom there are deeply thankful for this demonstration of solidarity with the exploited, the voiceless, and the powerless ones. The protest is not, might I point out, anti-South Africa. It is decidedly anti-apartheid, anti-injustice, anti-oppression, which are not the same thing.

It is one of the ironies of the South African situation that I can here, in this great and free land, the land of the brave and home of the free, address so august a body as this, the U.S. Senate; and yet, in my own country, the land of my birth, I would not be able to speak to a comparable body because I and nearly 23 million other black South Africans are victims of the politics of exclusion.

Here I am, a bishop in the church of God, 53 years of age, who some might even be ready to risk calling reasonably responsible, and yet I cannot vote in my motherland; whereas, a child of 18 years of age, because she is white, and only very recently colored and Indian, can vote. . . .

I have tried to engage the South African Government in dialogue, despite their unrelenting efforts to vilify and discredit the South African Council of Churches and its employees, despite the government's strictures that we were fomenting revolution at a time when the government was allegedly embarking on the road to reform. We reckoned the situation was too serious to try to be scoring debate points, and subsequent events have borne out our apprehensions.

The Nobel Peace Prize is a global indication of the South African Council of Churches and those associated with it that the world recognizes that we are true agents of justice, of peace, of reconciliation, and that we in the South African Council of Churches stand between South Africa and disaster. . . .

New Constitution

The new constitution is an instrument of the politics of

exclusion. Seventy-three percent of South Africa's population, the blacks, have no part in this constitution, which mentions them quite incredibly only once. How could this be seen as a step in the right direction? How could this be regarded as even remotely democratic? Its three chambers are racially defined. Consequently, racism and ethnicity are entrenched and hallowed in the constitution.

BISHOP DESMOND TUTU

Bishop Desmond Tutu, 1984 Nobel Peace Laureate, is an Anglican bishop and is general secretary of the South African Council of Churches. His voice is full of passion for change in his divided land. This outspoken 53 year old cleric is perhaps the most widely accepted black critic of apartheid permitted to operate in his country today

Source:
American Lutheran Church

In the parliamentary committees the composition is in the ratio of four whites to two coloreds to one Indian, and even if your arithmetic is bad, you know that two plus one can never equal let alone be more than four. Thus white minority rule is perpetuated and entrenched in this constitution.
Coloreds and Indians are being co-opted to perpetuate the oppression of the vast majority of South Africa's population.

Mercifully, they rejected this monumental hoax to hoodwink the world into thinking that South Africa's apartheid-mongers are changing—for only 20 percent of colored and Indians participated in the August elections. It has been a dangerous fiddling, while our Rome burnt.

The oppressed have protested this politics of exclusion and they have done so peacefully. They have staged stayaways and demonstrations against the new constitution, against sham black local government, against increases in rent, against increases in the general sales tax, against the inferior education foisted on blacks. The South African Government

71

has reacted violently and with a mailed fist—against a popular and mass movement of peaceful protest it has reacted with violence.

It has detained the leaders of the election boycott movement. It has arrested the leaders of the trade union movement who staged the most successful legal strike for political reasons, all without due process, without preferring charges, and having the evidence tested in open court. The writ of habeas corpus in many instances no longer exists in South Africa. . . .

Communism

I have said that blacks deplore communism as being atheistic and materialistic. But they would regard the Russians as their saviors, were they to come to South Africa, because anything in their view would be better than apartheid for the enemy of my enemy is my friend. When you were in a dungeon, and a hand is put out to unlock the door and get you out, you don't ask for the credentials of the owner of the hand. After all, the West was not too finicky in accepting the Russians as allies against Nazism.

Twenty-four blacks were killed during that 2-day strike in November. Six thousand were sacked from their jobs. There was not a squeak of protest from the Government of this country. When a priest in Poland went missing, and then his body was found, there was an outrage in this country and the media quite rightly gave it all extensive coverage. When 12 black South Africans are killed by the South African police, and 6,000 people are sacked, you are lucky if you get that much coverage. There was no expression of outrage and concern. That is part of constructive engagement.

I believe we are being told that this administration is not being soft on apartheid. Heaven help us when they do decide to be soft.

Would the reaction and the silence have been so deafening if the casualties had for instance been Jewish?

The South African Government has uprooted over 3 million blacks and dumped them as if they were rubbish in Bantustan homelands and not even an uncustomary protest by the State Department could stop them from uprooting 300 families from Mogopa. Just now a community, the people of Kwangena in the eastern Transvaal face the threat of being

> *I believe we are being told that this administration is not being soft on apartheid. Heaven help us when they do decide to be soft.*
>
> *Would the reaction and the silence have been so deafening if the casualties had been white? Would the reaction and the silence have been so deafening if the casualties had for instance been Jewish?*
>
> *The South African Government has uprooted over 3 million blacks and dumped them as if they were rubbish in Bantustan homelands.*

uprooted. It is the same community, one of whose leaders, Saul Mkhize, was killed protesting the removal of his people from Driefontein. . . .

Aggression and Violence

It is no use for South Africa entering into nonaggression pacts with foreign countries when it carries out acts of aggression against its own civilian population, when it sets the army on defenseless civilians. It is no use having detente only for external consumption when the South African Government refuses to talk with our real leaders inside the country and those in exile. For the problem of South Africa is not outside that country. The problem of South Africa is inside South Africa. The problem of South Africa is the system, the repressive and unjust system of apartheid.

Mr. Chairman, our people are peace loving to a fault. They have sought to change South Africa's racist policies by peaceful means since 1912 at the very least, using conventional peaceful methods of demonstrations, petitions, delegations, and even a passive resistance campaign. As a tribute to this commitment of our people to peaceful change, the only two South Africans to have won Nobel Peace Prizes are both of them black.

The response of the authorities, as I have said so many times before, has been police dogs, tear gas, guns, death, detention, and exile. Protesting peacefully against the past laws, 69 of our people in the Sharpville 1960 march were massacred, most of them shot in the back, running away. In 1976 our children protested peacefully against Bantu education, singing songs in the streets, and over 500 people were killed. Many of our children are in exile, most of whose whereabouts are unknown to their parents. Now in the most serious protest against apartheid, nearly 200 of our people have been killed, most by the authorities who are using the army, as I have said, against a peaceful civilian population, and the West does not appear to care.

Constructive engagement goes on. Namibia we were told 4 years ago would be independent because of constructive engagement. Namibia, 4 years later, is not independent. The United States has provided a recalcitrant South Africa with a further reason for dragging its feet by linking Namibian independence with the withdrawal of Cuban troops from a sovereign state, Angola, and in the meantime people are dying, people are suffering needlessly.

Constructive engagement has worsened our situation under apartheid. Four years ago I said this policy was an unmitigated disaster for us blacks. Four years later I have no reason to alter my original assessment despite what Dr. Chester Crocker is reported to have said.

It is giving democracy a bad name, just as apartheid has given free enterprise a bad name.

A Moral Issue

We are talking about a moral issue. You are either for or against apartheid, and not by rhetoric. You are either in favor of evil or you are in favor of good. You are either on the side of the oppressed or on the side of the oppressor. You cannot be neutral. Apartheid is evil, is immoral, is un-Christian, without remainder. It uses evil, immoral, and un-Christian methods. If you have supported the Nazis against the Jews, you would have been accused of adopting an immoral position. Apartheid is an evil as immoral and un-Christian in my view as Nazism, and in my view, the Reagan administration's support and collaboration with it is equally immoral, evil and totally un-Christian, without remainder.

In court you are guilty as an accessory before or after the fact. Constructive engagement is saying blacks are dispensable. Why should this administration respond so quickly and so decisively when something is done against Solidarity in Poland, applying sanctions at the drop of a hat, and yet when similar treatment is meted out to black trade unions in

South Africa, all we get is convoluted soph

America is a great country, with great trad
freedom and equality. I hope this great countr
to its history and its traditions, and will unequiv
clearly take its stand on the side of right and just
South Africa, for what the United States decides ar
has a crucial bearing on what happens in other lands
lives will be saved, many blacks will be won for demod
in South Africa if the United States is true to her real se

Constructive Engagement

I said 4 years ago that to protest constructive engagement
I would not see any representatives of the Reagan
administration. I relented because I thought I could persuade
them of the folly and the danger of constructive engagement, and because of an educational program for black
South Africans in which I was involved.

I have failed to persuade Dr. Crocker, a good and very
intelligent man, and others. So I want to state here that I will
not see anyone of the Reagan administration as of today
unless constructive engagement is abandoned. I may see the
President of this country or the Secretary of State if they do
invite me to meet with them.

I am deeply saddened. What have we still to say which we
have not said? What have we still to do which we have not
done to persuade people that all we want is to be recognized
for who we are, human, created in the image of God?

How must we say that we don't want to drive white people
into the sea, that we want to live amicably with them in a
nonracial, a truly democratic South Africa?

I hope this great country, with an extraordinary capacity
sometimes for backing the wrong horse, will for once break
that record. Will you please for a change listen to the victims
of oppression. We shall be free, and we will remember who
helped us to become free.

That is not a threat. It is just a statement of fact. We want
so desperately, so eagerly, to be friends with the United
States, after South Africa is liberated, for all its people, black
and white, as it shall.

\TION

ᴜn Mandela

Nelson Mandela is the leader of the African National Con-
gress (ANC). He was sentenced to life imprisonment at the
1964 Rivonia trial and has been held in prison for more than
20 years. The following comments are excerpted from
Nelson Mandela's Rivonia trial speech.

Points to Consider

1. How long did the African National Congress (ANC) pursue
   a policy of peaceful opposition to apartheid?
2. Why did the ANC turn to the use of violence?
3. What was their specific strategy for the use of violence?
4. How does the South African Government use violence?

Excerpt taken from *The Sun Will Rise - Statements from the Dock*
by Southern African Political Prisoners, edited by Mary Benson and
published by the International Defence and Aid Fund for Southern
Africa, London, 1981.

It may not be easy for this Court to understand, but it is a fact that for a long time the people had been talking of violence—of the day when they would fight the white man and win back their country, and we, the leaders of the ANC, had nevertheless always prevailed upon them to avoid violence and to pursue peaceful methods.

"I am the First Accused.

I hold a Bachelor's Degree in Arts and practiced as an attorney in Johannesburg for a number of years in partnership with Oliver Tambo. I am a convicted prisoner serving five years for leaving the country without a permit and for inciting people to go on strike at the end of May 1961.

At the outset, I want to say that the suggestion made by the State in its opening that the struggle in South Africa is under the influence of foreigners or communists is wholly incorrect. I have done whatever I have done, both as an individual and as a leader of my people, because of my experience in South Africa and my own proudly-felt African background, and not because of what any outsider might have said.

In my youth in the Transkei, I listened to the elders of my tribe telling stories of the old days. Amongst the tales they related to me were those of wars fought by our ancestors in defense of the fatherland. The names of Dingane and Bambata, Hintsa and Makana, Squngthi and Dalasile, Moshoeshoe and Sekhukhuni, were praised as the glory of the entire African nation. I hoped then that life might offer me the opportunity to serve my people and make my own humble contribution to their freedom struggle. This is what has motivated me in all I have done in relation to the charges made against me in this case. . . .

. . . Some of the things so far told to the Court are true and some are untrue. I do not, however, deny that I planned sabotage. I did not plan it in a spirit of recklessness, nor because I have any love of violence. I planned it as a result of a calm and sober assessment of the political situation that had arisen after many years of tyranny, exploitation and oppression of my people by the whites.

Source: E. Gentry for *The People*

I admit immediately that I was one of the persons who helped to form Umkhonto We Sizwe, and that I played a prominent role in its affairs until I was arrested in August 1962.

Strategy of Violence

. . . I and the others who started the organization did so for two reasons. Firstly, we believed that as a result of Government policy, violence by the African people had become inevitable, and that unless responsible leadership was given to canalise and control the feelings of our people, there would be outbreaks of terrorism which would produce an intensity of bitterness and hostility between the various races of this country which is not produced even by war. Secondly, we felt that without violence there would be no way open to the African people to succeed in their struggle against the principle of white supremacy. . . .

But the violence which we chose to adopt was not terrorism. We who formed Umkhonto were all members of the African National Congress, and had behind us the ANC tradition of non-violence and negotiation as a means of solving political disputes. We believed that South Africa belonged to all the people who lived in it, and not to one group, be it black or white. We did not want an interracial war, and tried to avoid it to the last minute. . . .

The African National Congress was formed in 1912 to defend the rights of the African people which had been seriously curtailed by the South Africa Act, and which were then being threatened by the Native Land Act. For thirty-seven years—that is, until 1949—it adhered strictly to a constitutional struggle. It put forward demands and resolutions; it sent delegations to the Government in the belief that African grievances could be settled through peaceful discussion and that Africans could advance gradually to full political rights. But white Governments remained unmoved, and the rights of Africans became less instead of becoming greater. In the words of my leader, Chief Luthuli, who became President of the ANC in 1952, and who was later awarded the Nobel Peace Prize:

'Who will deny that thirty years of my life have been spent knocking in vain, patiently, moderately and modestly at a closed and barred door? What have been the fruits of moderation? The past thirty years have seen the greatest number of laws restricting our rights and progress, until today we have reached a stage where we have almost no rights at all. . . .'

The ANC launched the Defiance Campaign, in which I was placed in charge of volunteers. This campaign was based on the principles of passive resistance. More than 8,500 people defied apartheid laws and went to jail. Yet there was not a single instance of violence in the course of this campaign on the part of any defier. I and nineteen colleagues were convicted for the role which we played in organizing the campaign, but our sentences were suspended mainly because the judge found that discipline and non-violence had been stressed throughout. . . .

In 1956, one hundred and fifty-six leading members of the Congress Alliance, including myself, were arrested on a charge of high treason and charges under the Suppression of Communism Act. The non-violent policy of the ANC was put in issue by the State, but when the Court gave judgement some five years later, it found that the ANC did not have a policy of violence. We were acquitted on all counts, which included a count that the ANC sought to set up a communist state in place of the existing regime. The government has always sought to have all its opponents as communists. This allegation has been repeated in the present case, but as I will show, the ANC is not, and never has been, a communist organization.

In 1960, there was the shooting at Sharpeville, which resulted in the proclamation of a state of emergency and the declaration of the ANC as an unlawful organization. My colleagues and I, after careful consideration, decided that we would not obey this decree . . . The ANC refused to dissolve, but instead went underground. We believed it was our duty to preserve this organization which had been built up with almost fifty years of unremitting toil. I have no doubt that no self-respecting white political organization would disband itself if declared illegal by a government in which it had no say. . . .

The Use of Violence

It may not be easy for this Court to understand, but it is a fact that for a long time the people had been talking of violence—of the day when they would fight the white man and win back their country, and we, the leaders of the ANC, had nevertheless always prevailed upon them to avoid violence and to pursue peaceful methods. When some of us discussed this in May and June of 1961, it could not be denied that our policy to achieve a non-racial state by non-violence had achieved nothing, and that our followers were beginning to lose confidence in this policy and were developing disturbing ideas of terrorism.

It must not be forgotten that by this time violence had, in fact, become a feature of the South African political scene. There had been violence in 1957 when the women of Zeerust were ordered to carry passes; there was violence in 1958 with the enforcement of cattle culling in Sekhukhuniland; there was violence in 1959 when the people of Cato Manor protested against pass raids; there was violence in 1960 when the Government attempted to impose Bantu Authorities in Pondoland. Thirty-nine Africans died in these disturbances. In 1961 there had been riots in Warmbaths, and all this time the Transkei had been a seething mass of unrest. Each disturbance pointed clearly to the inevitable growth among Africans of the belief that violence was the only way out—it showed that a Government which uses force to maintain its rule teaches the oppressed to use force to oppose it. Already small groups had risen in the urban areas and were spontaneously making plans for violent forms of political struggle. There now arose a danger that these groups would adopt terrorism against Africans, as well as whites, if not properly directed. . . .

After a long and anxious assessment of the South African situation, I and some colleagues came to the conclusion that as violence in this country was inevitable, it would be unrealistic and wrong for African leaders to continue preaching peace and non-violence at a time when the Government met our peaceful demands with force. . . .

Umkhonto We Sizwe (Spear of the Nation)

In the Manifesto of Umkhonto published on 16 December 1961, we said:

'The time comes in the life of any nation when there remain only two choices—submit or fight. That time has now come to South Africa. We shall not submit and we have no choice but to hit back by all means in our power in defense of our people, our future and our freedom'.

... Umkhonto was formed in November 1961. When we took this decision, and subsequently formulated our plans, the African National Congress heritage of non-violence and racial harmony was very much with us. We felt that the country was drifting towards a civil war in which blacks and whites would fight each other. We viewed the situation with alarm. Civil war could mean the destruction of what the ANC stood for; with civil war, racial peace would be more difficult than ever to achieve. We already have examples in South African history of the results of war. It has taken more than fifty years for the scars of the South African War to disappear. How much longer would it take to eradicate the scars of inter-racial war, which could not be fought without a great loss of life on both sides? ...

Four forms of violence are possible: sabotage, guerrilla warfare, terrorism and open revolution. We chose to adopt the first method and to exhaust it before taking any other decision. ...

Sabotage did not involve loss of life, and it offered the best hope for future race relations.

14 THE INTERNAL RESISTANCE

DECLARING WAR
ON APARTHEID

Oliver Tambo

*The following comments were excerpted from a transcript of
the press conference given by the African National Congress
President Oliver Tambo in Lusaka, Zambia, on June 25, 1985.
It is taken from* Zechaba, *the official journal of the African
National Congress (ANC).*

. . . .

*Question. The ANC (African National Congress) lays great
emphasis on unity. How do you see the question of unity
with such groups as PAC [Pan Africanist Congress] and
other small groupings inside South Africa?*

Answer: The ANC has always encouraged the unity of our
people inside the country. We have campaigned ceaselessly
for united action. We've called on our people in the various
organizational formations, in different political units, to fight
on their own fronts; but also to address the common enemy,
and to do so in unity with everybody else. That covers all
political organizations, all ideological trends. It addresses
the workers, the South African people as a whole who are
opposed to the racist system of education. That is why the
ANC was pleased, to say the least, when the UDF[1] was formed, because that created a platform exactly for united action.

Now and again there are slight differences, but by and
large the ANC pursues the position that whatever we differ

Excerpted from the August, 1985 issue of *Sechaba*.

[1] The United Democratic Front, formed in 1983, is a broad coalition of some
600 community groups, women's organizations, students associations, trade
unions, and other anti-apartheid organizations. The combined membership
of its components is nearly 2 million.

Source:
Tom Keough in
The Guardian

about, let us be united in defeating and destroying the apartheid regime. Some organizations, for example, don't quite accept every word that the Freedom Charter[2] says. We accept that. We continue to try to convince them that the Freedom Charter poses the alternative to the apartheid system; that there is no other answer. But, even when they differ with any article in the Freedom Charter—they still believe that the regime should be overthrown. On that basis we say—let us act together.

Q. *Your statement says that the Conference resolved the struggle must escalate. In the light of the SADF [South African Defense Force] aggression in Botswana, will the ANC be able to secure itself from such attacks?*

A. When we decided on armed struggle we accepted its consequences. It was a declaration of a readiness to sacrifice. On the other hand, when the regime persists in its apartheid system in the first instance, and also in killing our people, subjecting them to a succession of massacres, it also must accept the consequences of its actions. We have declared war on apartheid. The regime has declared war on all opponents of apartheid. But we declared war because apartheid was war against the people anyway.

---

[2] The Freedom Charter is a program of democratic demands for the abolition of the apartheid system, drawn up at a Congress of the People in Kliptown, South Africa, in June 1955. It has been adopted by the ANC as its program.

From 1948 when the Nationalist Party came into power it pursued policies which were a declaration of war on the people, on the international community. This has been particularly manifest during the last decade when the leaders of our region have complained of an undeclared war against their countries. So, the region is unavoidably in a state of continuing war of one degree or another, and it will be in that state of war until the war is ended. The war will end when the Nazis of our region are defeated by our people and the international community, which knows about Nazism.

Q. The regime has been making changes to some of the laws that govern the system—the Immorality Act, Transport, etc. Do you think that the changes taking place in South Africa will have an effect on the freedom struggle vis-a-vis the scaling down of the freedom struggle?

A. Apartheid expresses itself in many ways. Small ways, big ways. There is something fundamental about apartheid; there is something superficial. Not so long ago we were not allowed to go into the same lift (elevator).

When I say we, I mean Blacks—non-whites, as we were called. That restriction was removed. That was many years ago. Since then the struggle has waged on—apartheid has continued killing, it has even crossed its own borders and killed freely in Botswana, Lesotho, Swaziland, Mozambique, in Zimbabwe, Namibia, Angola, Seychelles, and in this country—it has continued despite the removal of that restriction, because the removal of the restriction of going into a lift was not what we were fighting about. We are not asking to be allowed to go into a lift with anybody. And the same thing applies to trains; now you can go into any compartment. That has nothing to do with what we are fighting about. . . .

Q. There have been reports in the run-up to the Conference, some allegedly well-sourced, which say that the ANC Conference might reconsider the movement's hesitancy in the past about hitting militarily what are termed soft targets. Did the Conference arrive at any closer definition of what it would regard as a legitimate military target?

A. I will summarize the position taken by the Conference in these terms: that the struggle must be intensified at all costs. Over the past 9 to 10 months at least—at the very least—there have been many soft targets hit by the enemy.

A National Movement

Q. Are you supported by the churches in your struggle?

A. The churches at one time worked together with the apartheid system. However, that is over, and they are now an element of the people's movement against apartheid.

Q. On the other hand, the ANC also has Communist and atheist members. Is this not a contradiction?

A. No, it is not a contradiction, because the ANC is not a party but a national movement. Our members are Communists and anti-Communists, Christians and Muslims. The ANC program laid down in our Freedom Charter unites us.

Oliver Tambo, Interview in Lusaka, August, 1985

Nearly 500 people have now died in that period. That works out at about 50 a month, massacred, shot down, killed secretly. All those were very, very soft targets. But they belong to this sphere of the intensification of the struggle because when people were killed they did not run away, they kept on at all costs, and went back into battle at all costs. In the process some innocent people were killed, some White, some Black. What we have seen in the Eastern Cape and places like that is what escalation means for everybody. The distinction between "soft" and "hard" is going to disappear in an intensified confrontation, in an escalating conflict. And when the regime sends its army across the borders to kill people in Botswana, including nationals of that country, and nationals of other countries, they are hitting soft targets —very soft, and not even in their own country.

That is not the end of the story. Exactly because of that the regime must be removed, at all costs. Therefore the struggle must be intensified, at all costs. The question of soft targets was quite out of place during World War II, to mention a big war. Ours will be a small one, but we are fighting the same kind of system. It was Hitler who attacked, it is the apartheid system here which attacked, and we are fighting that system, our own version of Nazism. I think the distinction between hard and soft targets is being erased by the development of the conflict. I am not saying that our Conference used the word soft targets. I am saying that the Conference recognized that we are in it. It is happening every day. It happened two days before we started our conference—a massacre in Gaborone [Botswana]. We did not complain that soft targets were being hit, because they have been hitting them, as I say, all the time. What we did was to re-commit ourselves to intensify our struggle until that kind of massacre, until the system which makes massacres and conflicts necessary, is abolished by mankind, and we stand ready to make the sacrifices necessary to achieve that objective. We call upon the African people everywhere to stand ready to play their role. We call on Africa and the international community to come to our aid and also play their part in getting rid of a system which is abhorrent to themselves. The struggle will be escalated.

Q. On your strategy of fighting: So far the ANC has been attacking only buildings . . . and offices, but avoiding attacks on the Whites themselves. Do you intend to change this strategy and start attacking the Whites . . . ?

A. That's not quite the correct presentation of our position. We have not been avoiding hitting Whites as Whites. There was no policy of hitting buildings instead of Whites. This is not the distinction that we have been making. If we have made any distinction it has been to avoid hitting people. But what I have said here is that in the course of intensification of the struggle the distinction between soft and hard targets—buildings and people—will naturally disappear. In the intensified situation, in the intensified conflict, in the course of escalation, that is not going to be avoidable. It has already happened. Amongst the 500 people I'm mentioning, there are many Whites who have been affected.

15 THE INTERNAL RESISTANCE

THE NEW CONSTITUTION: EXTENDING DEMOCRACY

The South African Government

The following comments are excerpted from a special publication on The New Parliament *issued by the South African Department of Foreign Affairs in November, 1984.*

Points to Consider

1. What role do blacks have in the new constitution?
2. How is the future of black political participation described?
3. How is the Parliament organized?
4. What racial groups have representation in the Parliament?
5. What powers do whites have in the government that other racial groups lack?

Excerpted from *The New Parliament*, November, 1984, a publication by the South African Department of Foreign Affairs.

Black people who live in the national and independent states already have political rights in their own geographical regions. In the metropolitan areas Black people have full political rights in local government.

September 1984 will be recorded in the annals of South African history as a month crowded with important events which had far-reaching effects on the country's constitutional development. The Republic of South Africa reached a significant phase in its political history during September of this year with the inauguration of its first executive State President, the opening of the country's first multiracial Parliament, and the swearing-in of the first South African Coloured and Indian Cabinet Ministers.

Pieter Willem Botha, a man who has left an indelible stamp on the process of constitutional change in South Africa, was inaugurated in office on September 14, 1984 with pomp and ceremony in the Mother City, Cape Town, as the Republic of South Africa's first executive State President . . . The new State President, a deeply religious man, accepted the burden of his new responsibilities and sought the blessing of the Almighty on his office. . . .

The events of September 1984 took place in an atmosphere of stately formality as befits an historic changeover from one form of government to another. The Westminster system of government which had been practiced since the establishment of the Union of South Africa in 1910 until recently, had become outdated in spite of the invaluable role which the system played for many years.

Through the years the unfolding of internal constitutional changes and political events had, however, brought the realization that the Westminster system had become obsolete in a multiracial society such as South Africa.

Racial Diversity

South Africa has a unique population composed of many racial minorities. It is a country with a wide diversity of peoples of divergent cultures, traditions and languages; communities which are at different stages of economic develop-

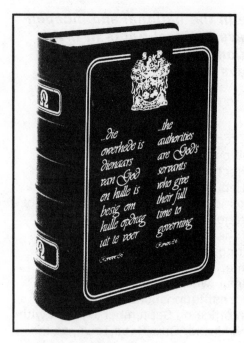

THE OATH
OF OFFICE

State President Botha took the oath of allegiance with his hand placed on the new State Bible

ment. In order to accommodate this great variety of races, South Africa had to find its own blueprint of acceptable government, applicable to its own unique situation and circumstances. The Westminster system had, therefore, to make way for a new constitutional dispensation which could meet the demands and realities of the country's unusual circumstances.

Since the early 1970s successive South African governments applied themselves diligently to the search for a new and more appropriate constitutional dispensation. The recently implemented Constitution is the culmination of many years of intensive consultation, hard work, and indepth investigations into the matter. The new Constitution resulted from the acceptance of the draft Constitution by a two-thirds majority in Parliament on September 9, 1983.

In a referendum held on November 2, 1983 the White electorate of South Africa accepted the new Constitutuion, also with a two-third majority of votes, in which provision is made for the composition of the first multiracial Parliament and Government. South Africa could, therefore, go ahead with the practical implementation of a government representative of the White, Coloured and Indian groups based on the principle of healthy powersharing.

Steps followed soon afterwards to put the new Constitution into practice. In August 1984 Coloured and Indian voters went to the polls to elect their own parliamentary representatives. Early in September the newly-chosen members took their seats in Parliament in Cape Town to take the oath of allegiance. The House of Assembly was retained unchanged, as the House which represents the Whites in the new dispensation. The new constitutional steps are considered to be the starting point only for further development. The first real, positive steps have been taken to establish a new form of government in practice. Future adaptations will be made as and when circumstances and developments merit the taking of such steps.

Urban Blacks

Insofar as the urban Black population is concerned, ongoing discussions and Cabinet attention is constantly directed towards these people and how they are to be accommodated in decision-making processes. Black people who live in the national and independent states already have political rights in their own geographical regions. In the metropolitan areas Black people have full political rights in local government. At this stage, however, no finality has yet been reached about how they will be accommodated in second tier government, namely, at provincial administration level, and at the highest level of the central government.

Political Reform

In opening the First Session of the Eighth Parliament of the Republic of South Africa on September 18, 1984, the State President said:

"Evolutionary and constitutional political reform found new meaning today. A constitutional dispensation in which different population groups have a political voice, without the domination of one group by another, begins here. This is another milestone on the road of South Africa, marked by historic beacons such as the creation of Union in 1910 and the establishment of a Republic in 1961.

Blacks Have Political Rights

Obviously it is correct to say that Blacks are not represented in central Government, but it is false to claim that Blacks have not rights. They have political rights at several levels. In the self-ruling national states, where 6,7-million people live, sophisticated Black government administrations have wide powers in respect of education, local government, police, agriculture, health and hospital services. These facts are ignored.

D.J. Louis Nel, South African Minister of Foreign Affairs, August 16, 1985

"Concrete form is today being given to the results of many years of aspirations to establish and extend the democratic process in a meaningful way for Coloureds and Indians, with the retention of stability. These groups, which had limited political rights in the past, hereby acquire a voice in the decision-making processes. Further meaning is therefore given to their citizenship."

With reference to participation by the Black people, the State President said:

"Politically, Black participation requires structures and processes other than those offered by this constitution. We therefore realize that the Constitution in terms of which this Parliament has been created, and by which you have been summoned here today, does not provide fully for the diversity which marks the South African population. Democratic political participation must also be further extended among our Black communities in South Africa in order to ensure their advancement and to meet the demands for justice.

"My Government will continue to create, on the basis of consultation and negotiation, a framework within which co-operation with Black States, both independent and self-governing, can take place. Furthermore, means will have to be found to enable Black communities outside the independent and self-governing states, to participate in political decision-making in matters affecting their interests. Thus we must continue to build on the foundations which were laid by the establishment of Black local authorities."

President Botha continued:

"Our gathering here today indicates a continuance along the road we have chosen here at the southern tip of Africa to establish a society which will ensure peace, prosperity and justice for all, and which honors the right to self-determination for all of the country's population groups and nations.

"Today we affirm our aspirations to maintain Christian values and civilized norms, with the preservation of freedom of religion.

Structure of the Government

The executive State President is the Head of State, chosen by an electoral college for the same period of time as Parliament. He serves as chairman of the Cabinet, but is not a member of any of the three Houses that comprise Parliament.

The Cabinet is appointed by the State President from members of all three population groups, Whites, Coloureds and Indians, who are represented in Parliament. The Cabinet has executive powers in matters of general interest, such as defense, finance, and foreign affairs. . . .

Parliament comprises three Houses, each of which consists of members elected by the population group concerned as their representatives for a term of five years. Parliament has legislative authority in matters of general affairs which have been approved by all three Houses.

There are 178 White members of the Assembly, 85 Coloured members of the House of Representatives; and 45 Indian members of the House of Delegates. The majority of members are chosen in a general election; a few only are directly appointed.

Joint standing committees, comprising members of all three Houses, including members of Opposition parties, are appointed. It will be their function to try to bring about consensus on all matters of common interest, including legislation. If consensus cannot be achieved, the State President has the power to refer any point of dispute to the Presidents' Council for a ruling. It could, however, also happen that the State President, in deliberation with the Cabinet or the Ministers' Councils could find a solution to such a dispute.

When choosing a new State President an electoral college is appointed consisting of 88 members of Parliament, of whom 50 are from the House of Assembly, 25 from the House of Representatives; and 13 from the House of Delegates. The college is chosen from members of the majority parties in each House. . . .

The Speaker of Parliament is the chairman of the full Parliament, and the choice rests with him as to where he wishes to take the chair on a specific day. He is the chairman of all joint sessions of the three Houses, which sessions can only be called by the State President and the Speaker. When the Speaker is not in the chair in a specific House, the assembly is led by the chairman of the particular House.

As is the case in the House of Assembly, there is a Leader of the Opposition in the House of Representatives and in the House of Delegates, as well as a Chief Whip for each party represented in the Houses.

Legislation

Each House will decide by majority vote—without interference from outside—on legislation affecting only the affairs of that specific population group. The State President is obliged to approve such laws after they have been passed by the House in question.

Legislation on general or national affairs must be approved by all three Houses in separate session before they go to the State President for approval. The President's Council may, however, give a decision in cases where there is disagreement among the different Houses.

16 THE INTERNAL RESISTANCE

ELECTION REFORMS:
A CRUEL HOAX

Tafataona P. Mahoso

The author is a professor of African and modern world history at Rutgers University in Camden, New Jersey.

Points to Consider

1. How does the Reagan administration deal with apartheid?
2. What are the major racial groups in South Africa?
3. How does the new constitution deal with these major racial groups?
4. How has the Reagan Administration helped the apartheid system?

Tafataona P. Mahoso, "South African Elections," *Daily World*, September 13, 1984.

The biggest objection to the so-called reforms is that they leave out completely the overwhelming majority of 23 million Africans out of a total population of 30 million.

The Reagan administration and the Botha government in South Africa hope that the cruel hoax called "Colored (mixed nationality) and Indian Elections" will make the world believe that apartheid is reforming itself out of existence.

According to the U.S. State Department's Alan Romberg, the elections in South Africa are not just "a turn in the right direction" but actual evidence of the white minority regime's "commitment to reform we (the U.S.) consider so vital."

The only thing Romberg considers unfortunate about the elections is that the regime has detained almost all the leaders of the movement to boycott the vote. While the arrests are a gross violation of human rights, they are only a symptom of what is reprehensible about the entire exercise and the entire system called apartheid. Romberg regrets the arrest and detentions because they betray the fraudulent nature of the whole exercise, making it impossible to give apartheid a metropolitan facelift.

The Apartheid System

The South African regime, representing 4½ million descendants of Dutch and British settlers, had divided the country's population of 30 million into 23 million indigenous Africans, 2.6 million Coloreds, 850,000 Asians and, of course, Europeans.

Under the apartheid system dictated by whites, each ethnic group must occupy its own separate area and institutions. The white minority reserves to itself the best-watered, most fertile, and most minerally endowed 87% of the land area. The Asians and Coloreds live in segregated areas within that 87%. The 23 million Africans, however, have land and citizenship rights only in the most barren 13% of the land which the regime has further divided into about a dozen concentration settlements called bantustans.

By calling each of those reservations an independent nation, racist South Africa claims to have liberated the

Drawn by YURI CHEREPANOV in *Pravda*

indigenous Africans, so that the only groups entitled to consideration within "white" South Africa are the Coloreds and Indians, whom the whites have always tried to keep separate and use as a buffer between African and European. That is why under the so-called new constitution of South Africa only the Coloreds and Asians are granted the fake elections.

Africans work everywhere in South Africa, but only with the status of foreigners. They must carry passes which must be certified or decertified by white employers at their convenience. A decertified African must leave the white areas immediately, under threat of arrest and jail, for whatever area the regime considers his "tribal" bantustan.

Elections

What about the elections? Are they really a constructive reform, a move forward in the right direction? In fact they are a move backwards. In 1928 in Cape Province, one of four provinces of South Africa, a limited Black vote was granted, based on educational and property qualifications. However, Blacks could vote for white candidates only. In 1956 the Coloreds were placed on a separate voters' roll to elect a Colored Representative Council, made up of whites only, to "represent" the Coloreds in the all-white parliament. Africans too got an all-white Native Representative Council in 1936. The Native Council was abolished in 1959 and the Colored in 1968. Since that time all Black people have not had even a token of representation in the white parliament.

When whites abolished all tokens of Black representation in South Africa, the rest of the continent was coming under African majority rule won by parties educated and inspired in their struggles by the African National Congress (ANC) of South Africa. . . .

Since the main purpose of the apartheid state is to suppress African insurrection so as to continue the exploitation of African cheap labor, all police and military units must be staffed and officered by mostly white males. Africans cannot be trusted with the machinery of their own oppression. Therefore white males aged 17 to 60 are now drafted indefinitely, wreaking havoc upon an economy in which up to 23 job categories used to be reserved for whites only.

New Strategy

A new strategy was needed therefore, and in 1980 the future looked very bright for the apartheid regime: in both Britain and the United States there were conservative administrations willing to work to rehabilitate white South Africa in the eyes of the international community.

First, Reagan withdrew U.S. support for UN Resolution 435, which calls for South African withdrawal from Namibia to be followed by UN-supervised elections.

Second, Reagan revived the old South African gimmick of arguing that South African troops should not stop occupying and tormenting Namibia until Cuban troops stopped protecting Angola against South African attacks on that new nation.

Excluding the Majority

Black South Africans see it differently. The new constitution totally excludes the African majority, some 22 million people who make up 72 percent of the population, from any role in the national government. What is new is that Coloureds (2.7 million of mixed race) and Indians (875,000) will be included in a tricameral parliament.

Gail Hovey, *American Committee on Africa,* 1984

Third, Reagan changed the U.S. part of the UN arms embargo against South Africa, so that things like U.S. military transport planes exported to South Africa would no longer be regarded as weapons. The result was that South Africa received more arms from the U.S. in the first three years of Reagan than it had received in the past thirty years.

The fourth major help came to South Africa in the form of a $1 billion loan from the International Monetary Fund to help the regime cope with foreign exchange shortages and with the recession resulting from its war expenditures.

Then South Africa launched brutal military attacks on its neighbors while they were suffering from prolonged droughts, thereby forcing them to sign so-called nonaggression pacts under duress. The Reagan administration offered to promote these pacts overseas as proof of South Africa's peacemaking.

Finally, Reagan adopted foreign policy language which defined the freedom fighters of Namibia and South Africa as terrorists while the state which terrorized them was portrayed as the peacemaker.

New Constitution

To help the metropolitan powers in this campaign, South Africa had to make it look as if the racist system of apartheid was being reformed. Certain beaches, hotels and holiday resorts would be specifically exempt from racial segregation and given maximum press. The "Colored elections" represented some token constitutional changes. But these constitutional changes are no better than a return to the Colored Representative Council abolished in 1968. . . .

The biggest objection to the so-called reforms is that they leave out completely the overwhelming majority of 23 million Africans out of a total population of 30 million.

The purpose of these exercises is neither reform nor recognition of Black rights. The purpose is to co-opt two buffer groups, the Asians and the Coloreds, into closer collaboration with the apartheid state to maintain its ability to exploit the 23 million indigenous Africans. The purpose is to sow the most vicious suspicion between these two groups and the majority.

The first privilege which the children of the Coloreds and Asians will enjoy after the token elections will be their compulsory draft into apartheid's armies to fight both the African National Congress and the South West African People's Organization.

In other words, the so-called reforms are the latest open admission of the failure of the vision of a white southern Africa which both the South African High Commissioner and Henry Kissinger espoused. Fortunately for the forces of liberation, these reforms have already failed. Only 58% of the eligible Colored population registered to vote. Only 30% of the 58% actually voted, most of them coerced by police and employers in isolated areas. This means that only 17% of the eligible population voted, giving a boycott rate of 83%. The Asian boycott might be even higher when their turn comes up.

The hoax in South Africa convinced nobody except sponsors of racism.

WHAT IS EDITORIAL BIAS?

This activity may be used as an individualized study guide for students in libraries and resource centers or as a discussion catalyst in small group and classroom discussions.

The capacity to recognize an author's point of view is an essential reading skill. The skill to read with insight and understanding involves the ability to detect different kinds of opinions or bias. Sex bias, race bias, ethnocentric bias, political bias and religious bias are five basic kinds of opinions expressed in editorials and all literature that attempts to persuade. They are briefly defined in the glossary below.

5 Kinds of Editorial Bias

*sex bias— *the expression of dislike for and/or feeling of superiority over the opposite sex or a particular sexual minority*

*race bias— *the expression of dislike for and/or feeling of superiority over a racial group*

*ethnocentric bias—the expression of a belief that one's own group, race, religion, culture or nation is superior. Ethnocentric persons judge others by their own standards and values.

*political bias—the expression of political opinions and attitudes about domestic or foreign affairs

*religious bias—the expression of a religious belief or attitude

Guidelines

1. From the readings in chapter two, locate five sentences that provide examples of editorial opinion or bias.

2. Write down each of the above sentences and determine what kind of bias each sentence represents. Is it sex bias, race bias, ethnocentric bias, political bias or religious bias?

3. Make up one sentence statements that would be an example of each of the following: *sex bias, race bias, ethnocentric bias, political bias* and *religious bias.*

4. See if you can locate five sentences that are factual statements from the readings in chapter two.

5. What is the editorial message of the cartoon by Steve Kelley?

CHAPTER 3

CORPORATE DIVESTMENT

THE SULLIVAN PRINCIPLES ARE WORKING

Sal Marzullo

Sal Marzullo is the chairman of the Industry Support Unit for the Sullivan Principles devised by the Reverend Leon Sullivan, a veteran civil rights activist. In 1977 Sullivan developed a voluntary code of conduct for U.S. companies operating in South Africa, which pledges them to desegregate their facilities and pay equal wages to blacks. Currently 135 companies, including General Motors Corporation, Mobil Oil Corporation and virtually every other major U.S. employer in that country, are signatories to the Sullivan Principles.

Points to Consider

1. How have the Sullivan Principles promoted change and progress for blacks?
2. How many American companies have signed the Sullivan Principles?
3. What action has the South African business community taken regarding black employees?
4. What effect would divestment have?

Excerpted from testimony of Sal Marzullo before the U.S. Senate Banking, Housing and Urban Affairs Committee, June, 1985.

American companies have helped to accelerate reform and the Sullivan principles, far from being cosmetic, have been a useful vehicle for helping to build a climate for change.

Apartheid has been eroded by economic growth. The process of urbanization and industrialization has done more to doom traditional apartheid and separate development than any other single influence. If South Africa is to survive and prosper, we must build on that momentum and help to bring white and black South Africa together as one people, one nation. American companies have helped to accelerate reform and the Sullivan principles, far from being cosmetic, have been a useful vehicle for helping to build a climate for change—first in the workplace and later in the larger outside community. It has not been easy—it will not be easy in the future; but the changes are real and if apartheid has not yet been dismantled, its pillars have been hammered away and chipped at. It will ultimately fall. The growth of black trade unionism, for example, aided by U.S. companies, has provided one of the most fundamental changes to have taken place in South Africa so far. We should be seeking not to stop or impede the flow of this force for change, but to encourage it and provide incentives for it. Harry Oppenheimer, one of South Africa's leading industrialists and liberal spokesmen —as a matter of fact, he is one of the founders and backers of the PFP, the leading opposition party—has written that punitive acts, however well intentioned, may compromise the successes of the past and be counterproductive.

The Sullivan principles are not perfect. We keep revising them and Dr. Sullivan, a deeply committed man who has given so much of his total energies to this task, prods and pushes us and proposes still more challenges, and I suspect he will continue to do so. South Africa is not the same country it was just 5 years ago, and never will be again. Whatever its problems, the Sullivan principles have helped to shape major changes in South African legislation and labor policy. Changes have come both from internal forces now operative in the South African ambience—primarily the economic forces of South Africa's economic development—and from moral pressure from American shareholders, churches, and

Career center in Soweto for high school students.

Source: *South African Panorama*

others here in our own country. The responsible, concerned, caring pressure is welcome and has been productive. The simplistic sloganizing doesn't help very much.

Solution to Apartheid

We know, as you do, that the Sullivan principles alone are not a guaranteed method of providing quick and simple resolution of the injustices that exist in South African society. Only South Africans, all of them, will evolve the final solutions to their problems. But we must help them. In short, we strongly believe that our collective commitment to the Sullivan principles, properly coordinated and properly implemented, offers the possibility of making a greater contribution to change than does withdrawal. Again, I emphasize the vital importance not only of the changes but of their symbolic value. Our efforts are multiplied by those of leading South African businessmen and by South Africa's major employer groups who in January publicly committed themselves to a full and equal role for blacks in both the economic and political life of South Africa. These groups represent more than 80 percent of the employment strength of the country.

I might add here that since 1977, when 12 American signatory companies signed the original principles, we now total 152 companies. We have spent well over $100 million in health, education, community development, training, housing since 1978. More importantly, programs initially developed on a local level have now been developed for longer term results at both the regional and national levels in the fields of health, education, housing, and black entrepreneurship. We are making progress.

U.S. firms in South Africa are an anti-apartheid force, a force for change, for bridge building and racial reconciliation. Our severest critic in the United States, Reverend Sullivan himself, has said while calling for a complete end to apartheid the following:

"The principles are not an academic response designed to advance the views of those who are proponents of either investment or divestment. To the contrary, the principles are a pragmatic policy based upon the most judicious engagement of available resources, and are intended to improve the quality of life, to help bring justice to unliberated people, and to help build a peaceful, free South Africa for everyone."

We are at a critical juncture in South African history. Many white South Africans now understand that meaningful advance of the nonwhite population and their own long-term survival are not possible without fundamental structural reform of that society. We must work with these poeple to hasten the pace and to make those changes South Africans of all races desire. It would be ironic if at this critical point in South Africa's political history, when a government is beginning the process of fundamental change that we have all been calling for, that we who detest apartheid and all that it represents should make it impossible for those changes to take place peacefully.

The apartheid policies of South Africa are repugnant to all Americans. The debate, however, is not about defending apartheid, for it is indefensible. It destroys whites just as surely as it destroys blacks. The argument is about how

Improving Conditions for Blacks

The Sullivan principles are working. As a result of the principles, U.S. plants are desegregated, equal pay for equal work is beginning to be paid to black workers, blacks are being elevated to administrative and supervisory jobs, blacks are supervising whites, blacks are being trained with new technical skills, independent free black trade unions are being recognized, schools are being built, housing developments are being constructed, health centers and programs are being initiated and young blacks by the thousands are being assisted with better education.

Rev. Leon H. Sullivan, *Knight-Ridder Newspapers*, May 19, 1985

most effectively to change South Africa's racial policies and on that strategy good and honest men may and do disagree.

Conclusion

I would like to make the following points:

One, our only leverage to accomplish change in South Africa is in our presence. Withdrawal from South Africa would neither bring down the South African Government nor affect the policies of that Government.

Two, American firms, through adherence to voluntary standards of social responsibility, have been a leading force for evolutionary change away from apartheid. Mandatory, confrontational legislation would jeopardize that effort.

Three, divestment or curbing American investment would be against the wishes of a large number of South African blacks who see the role of U.S. business in their country as constructive and progressive.

Four, economic power is vital to the nonwhite community in South Africa. Investment, through jobs and training, provides that power. A well-educated and well-trained work force is the ultimate force causing the system to change.

Five, U.S. businesses should be encouraged to increase their role in the economy and their voluntary efforts to influence social change.

Six, to the extent that sanctions seek to govern the actions of South African affiliates of U.S. companies, they place these companies in an impossible situation between two authorities.

Seven, enactment of economic sanctions also would set a senseless precedent for subsequent legislation restricting U.S. business operations in any countries whose social policies might be objectionable. Not that this is the intent of the Senate, but all I'm saying is that I think we need to be very careful about how we put American business in a position where it is faced with competing authorities on an issue that's as delicate as this is. Certainly, we have every right as a country to protest infringements of human rights anywhere they exist.

THE SULLIVAN PRINCIPLES
HAVE FAILED

Jean Sindab

Jean Sindab is the executive director of the Washington Office on Africa (WOA), a research arm of the Free South Africa Movement. WOA is sponsored by some U.S. churches and trade unions.

Points to Consider

1. How many black people do U.S. corporations employ?
2. How do U.S. corporations eliminate unskilled jobs for blacks?
3. Why have trade unions in Africa been critical of the Sullivan Principles?
4. How is Mobil Oil Corporation's role in South Africa described?

Excerpted from testimony by Jean Sindab before the House Foreign Affairs Subcommittee on Africa, January 31, 1985.

Are the Sullivan Principles effective for the black workers these firms do employ? They have been so ineffective that an official of the Federation of South African Trade Unions (FOSATU) called them "window dressing on a broken window" when he was in Washington.

We are told that U.S. corporations are a "progressive force" for change in South Africa and that disinvestment would hurt black South Africans the most. We are told that a growing South African economy will ultimately help black South Africans financially and will lead to "reforms" in apartheid. Central to the "progressive force" argument is the adoption by U.S. corporations of the Sullivan Principles code of conduct. . . .

What of the Sullivan Principles? Are U.S. corporate practices a liberalizing influence in South Africa? The answer is no. U.S. corporations employ only 70,000 blacks (including "Coloureds" and "Asians")—only one percent of the total black workforce. Even if they wanted to be a good influence, the impact on the South African economic and political system would be negligible. Many of these corporations are making increasingly capital-intensive investments which eliminate unskilled jobs through automation. Blacks are concentrated in these types of unskilled jobs, while whites are concentrated in the technical, managerial positions which run the economy.

Largest Investors

An examination of some of the largest U.S. investors is telling. For example, Burroughs Corporation is the fourth largest U.S. investor in South Africa, yet it employs a total of 563 workers—only 55 of whom are African! Other computer corporations are similar. Mobil Oil is the largest U.S. investor, yet less than a third of its workers are African. Fluor employs only ten Africans out of 182 total workers. Ford and General Motors both employ a larger number of "Coloureds," but they also employ more whites than Africans.

Source: *CALC Report,* April, 1985

Are the Sullivan Principles effective for the black workers
these firms do employ? They have been so ineffective that
an official of the Federation of South African Trade Unions
(FOSATU) called them "window dressing on a broken window" when he was in Washington. Emma Mashinini, General
Secretary of the independent Commercial, Catering and
Allied Workers Union of South Africa called the Principles
"just good cosmetics for the outside world. To us trade
unionists, we see no difference between American and
South African companies." The Principles, even if they were
complied with, do nothing about the system of "grand
apartheid"—the pass laws, the "bantustans," forced
removals, the lack of the vote—and the security state that
enforces it. In a rare admission, even Rev. Sullivan himself
said last spring: "Even if all of the American companies
complied, we could not attain our objective of eliminating
apartheid." The struggle in South Africa is not about who
eats lunch with whom, it is about self-determination and
power. As Bishop Tutu said in July 1983: "The Sullivan Principles . . . are there to help make apartheid more acceptable,
more comfortable; and we do not want apartheid made more
comfortable, we want apartheid dismantled."

Two Case Studies

It is instructive to look at a couple of case studies. I have chosen Ford Motor Company and Mobil Oil. This is for several reasons: first, William Broderick of Ford and Sal Marzullo of Mobil Oil have been in the forefront of the corporate anti-divestment forces; second, these two corporations are among the largest U.S. investors and employers in South Africa; and third, they have consistently obtained glowing ratings from Rev. Sullivan's group.

Ford began its South African operations in 1923. For the 54 years between that time and 1977 when the Sullivan code was implemented, Ford contributed to the growth of the automotive industry in South Africa while simultaneously exploiting cheap black labor. It sold vehicles to South Africa's military and police. Only when the pressure mounted from the black South African trade union movement and the U.S. divestment movement did Ford and the other corporations design and sign on to the Principles in 1977.

Yet, just two weeks ago, eight years after the Principles were instituted and Ford became a signatory, an official of the National Automotive and Allied Workers Union (NAAWU), which represents some of Ford's workers, said that Ford is at the bottom of the payscale for black workers in the South African auto industry. In January 1982, the Motor Assemblers' and Component Workers Union of South Africa (MACWUSA), which represents workers at Ford's Port Elizabeth factory, called the Sullivan code a "toothless package" of "piecemeal reform that allows this cruel system of apartheid to survive." The union went on and evaluated Ford in each of the six Sullivan Principles, concluding that the Principles "circle around apartheid's basic structures," seeking "merely to modernize and ensure its perpetuation."

Ford's response to the November 1979 strike at its Struandale Port Elizabeth plant was also telling. The company fired 700 workers for walking off their jobs in protest of racist treatment by white management and white workers. Although Ford eventually reinstated the workers after tense negotiations, the South African security police conveniently detained several strike leaders, including Thozamile Botha, who was subsequently banned. A Carter Administration official said at the time that the Ford strike had sent "twenty rounds of buckshot into the Sullivan Principles." In an audit commissioned by Ford, the South African Institute of Race Relations reported in February 1980 that wage differentials at Ford "make a mockery of the Sullivan Principles. Yet, according to Rev. Sullivan, Ford is "making good progress."

Mobil is the seventh largest U.S. employer and the largest U.S. investor in South Africa. The company began operations in South Africa in 1897. Mobil's role in supporting the South African security state has best been described by the corporation itself. In response to an inquiry made by the United Church of Christ in the mid-1970s on the company's involvement in South Africa, Mobil replied that it could not provide that information. "Oil supplies are the very lifeblood of the army, navy, and airforce," Mobil's attorneys argued, and information about refining, storage, reserves, and distribution is "of the utmost strategic importance to the State." Oil falls within the South African legal definition of "munitions of war."

In 1980, some of our sponsoring churches filed a shareholders' resolution with Mobil to cease all sales to the South African military and police. Mobil responded:

"Total denials of supplies to the police and military forces of a host country is hardly consistent with an image of good citizenship in that country.

"The great bulk of the work of both the police and the military forces in every country, including South Africa, is for the benefit of all of its inhabitants. All have a basic interest in the maintenance of public order and safety."

This says it well. Mobil seeks to maintain the "order" of white minority rule and oppression. It sees no problem in supporting a police force known the world over for shooting peaceful protestors in the back. It is "good citizenship" to aid a military force illegally occupying Namibia and invading and destabilizing neighboring countries. Mobil Oil seeks to maintain the status quo of racist apartheid to continue reaping huge profits.

Let me repeat: I have chosen Ford and Mobil because they are supposedly the best. Our State Department calls them "the good guys." Over 150 corporations are not signatory to the Principles. Many of the ones who have signed do not file reports or receive failing grades. Some of the reports are incomplete because the South African Protection of Business Bill of 1978 states that companies cannot give information about their activities without the permission of the Minister of Economic Affairs. Corporations like Ford and Mobil support the Sullivan Principles because it is a useful public relations exercise that they hope will counter the economic impact of the divestment movement. . . .

Two Largest Unions

I would like to call your attention to the brave stance of the two largest black trade union federations in South Africa in favor of disinvestment—despite the real threat from the regime to the safety of their organizations and leaders. The Federation of South African Trade Unions (FOSATU) issued a statement in June 1984 stating that "the pressure for disinvestment has had a positive effect and should therefore not be lessened. FOSATU is definitely opposed to foreign investment that accepts the conditions of oppression maintained by this regime." The Council of Unions of South Africa (CUSA) issued a statement in December 1984 in favor of "selective disinvestment," targeting the corporations that provide strategic support to the maintenance of apartheid. Both trade union federations have spoken out against the Sullivan Principles.

A CALL FOR DIVESTMENT

John Ray

John Ray made this statement as a council member at large for the Council of the District of Columbia before the House Committee on the District of Columbia.

Points to Consider

1. Why is it wrong to invest in South Africa?
2. What are the two major arguments against divestiture or divestment?
3. Why would divestment not harm black employment in South Africa?
4. How does U.S. policy toward Poland and South Africa differ?

Excerpted from testimony by John Ray before the House Committee on the District of Columbia, January 31 and February 7, 1984.

*Some argue that divestiture amounts to nothing
more than an empty gesture with no force in
increasing the pressure for an end to apartheid. If
that is true, why does the South African government call it treason for its citizens to advocate the
withdrawal of U.S. investment? For a South
African to call for divestment is a crime punishable by prison or even death.*

Thank you for the opportunity to discuss the South Africa
divestiture bill enacted by the District of Columbia Council.

As principal sponsor of the bill, and as chairman of the
Council committee which managed it, I believe I can provide
useful information about the probable effects of the bill and
the reasons the Congress should allow it to become law.

The reasons are many. But one is overriding and, to my
mind, beyond question. It is wrong to invest in South Africa.
It is wrong as a matter of moral principle to invest in the
only nation on the earth which holds 20 million black people
in a state of near slavery. It is wrong to prop up the only
remaining nation on earth which, by law, denies basic human
rights to the majority of its population, for no reason other
than the color of their skin.

Withdrawing from South Africa is the right thing to do.
Putting aside all of the other arguments that can be made,
the rightness of this action is—and ought to be—compelling.

With the moral imperative clearly in mind, let me describe
exactly what the bill would do and why I am convinced it is
financially sound.

The bill would prohibit the District government from
investing public funds—the tax dollars of our citizens—in
banks and corporations which do business in South Africa or
Namibia. It would allow the government two years to divest
its present holdings in South Africa-related institutions. And
if divestiture could not be accomplished in two years, the
bill authorizes the Council to extend the time. . . .

FREE SOUTH AFRICA
DIVEST NOW
BREAK ECONOMIC LINKS WITH APARTHEID

Source: *The Militant*

Two Policy Arguments

Let me briefly address two policy arguments that have been raised and probably will be offered here today.

Some argue that divestiture amounts to nothing more than an empty gesture with no force in increasing the pressure for an end to apartheid. If that is true, why does the South African government call it treason for its citizens to advocate the withdrawal of U.S. investment? For a South African to call for divestment is a crime punishable by prison or even death.

Despite the danger, some have had the courage to call as strongly as they dare for the withdrawal of U.S. economic support for apartheid. Bishop Desmond Tutu, general secretary of the South African Council of Churches, has repeatedly risked his life and freedom to say as clearly as he can that the withdrawal of foreign investment is an essential step to bring about justice for all of South Africa's citizens.

If divestiture has no impact, why did the South African government pay a Washington law firm $300,000 to lobby against the Massachusetts divestment bill? And why did that same law firm, with the South African embassy as its client, assign an attorney to monitor the District of Columbia bill from almost the moment it was introduced?

Some opponents of the bill go a step further and argue that withdrawing American investments will actually harm black people in South Africa. They talk of the jobs American companies provide, and the example of racial integration that American companies are setting.

A quick look at the figures shows how absurd the argument is. American firms account for fewer than one per cent of all jobs in South Africa. Blacks hold only a small share of that one per cent, the share at the lowest level of pay.

With all due respect to Congressman Crane and others who play his music and sing his song, I must object to their failure to acknowledge the exploitation of the black labor force in South Africa. Mr. Crane, in his statement to the House on November 15, noted that "230,000 black laborers enter the South African labor market annually and by the end of the century, the number will rise to 360,000." It is interesting to observe the reference to "black laborers." Not black accountants, or lawyers, or presidents of corporations. As Mr. Crane well knows, blacks in South Africa are locked onto the lowest rung of the economic ladder, by the order of small-minded men who exalt color over all else.

But it is a mistake to allow Mr. Crane and other opponents of divestiture to cast the issue as a simple labor-management clash over jobs and wages. If full employment for blacks is the goal, the solution is easy. We need look no further than the American South a little more than a hundred years ago. It was called slavery.

The issue is not full employment. The issue is human rights, the most basic rights of the citizens of a nation to vote and speak freely, to stand on an equal footing in shaping the policies of their country, and to determine the course of their own lives.

U.S. Corporate Investment

"Literally, without U.S. corporate investment, Pretoria could not run its very expensive and complex apartheid system," Dr. Jean Sindab, director of the Washington Office on Africa (WOA), told the lawmakers. She explained that U.S. firms account for 70% of the funds invested in the South African computer business, 44% of the petroleum market and 20% of the automobile industry.

Jack Colhoun, *Guardian*, February 13, 1985

If all of us here today were unfortunate enough to be living in South Africa, most of us—whether black or white—would be in prison or dead merely for raising the arguments we freely raise here. I would not be here as a member of the legislative body of the nation's capital. The Chairman and several of the distinguished members of this Committee would not be here as elected representatives in this Congress.

A Double Standard

South Africa is very far away in miles. But we do not have to cross an ocean to understand what it means to be denied our rights because we are black.

Not long ago, Americans were roused to anger when a Communist government deprived the Polish people of their right to organize a labor movement. The Reagan administration imposed 11 different economic sanctions against Poland as a means of bringing pressure for reform. Like most Americans, I supported the government's actions against the Polish regime.

But I was dismayed that this government could object with such vigor to a denial of rights based on a difference in political philosophy—while ignoring South Africa's equally severe denial of rights based on race. We are told that South Africa practices Western-style democracy. Yet to grant or deny basic human rights according to the color of a man's skin runs counter to everything democracy means.

Even in the Soviet Union, the government and the Communist Party do not exclude citizens because of the color of their skin. One can choose to be a good Communist no matter what his racial or ethnic heritage.

But in South Africa, black people cannot be patriots of the government no matter how much they love their country. The government refuses even to acknowledge their citizenship, much less accord them equal rights in their land.

By enacting this bill, the District of Columbia Council has taken the strongest possible action available to us. We have charted a course which is right morally, and prudent financially. We have done no more than we are authorized to do by the law and the Constitution.

U.S. Foreign Policy

To those who argue that we are interfering with America's foreign policy, let me point out that the action of the District of Columbia affects only the public funds of the District of Columbia. We have not attempted to influence the spending of federal government money, because the Constitution forbids us to do that. But the Constitution does not require us, as individuals or as the elected legislature of this city, to rubber-stamp the policies of the national administration.

There are those in the Congress who claim that they support the right of Connecticut or other jurisdictions to take such action. But when it comes to the District of Columbia, they suddenly have doubts. If they question our honesty, let them come out and say it. If they doubt our integrity, let them say it. But if they are pretending to righteousness on one hand, while trying also to appease the corporate supporters of apartheid, let that be clearly recognized. We have had enough of politicians who straddle both sides of an issue.

Like the legislatures of Connecticut and Philadelphia and other states and cities, the Council of the District of Columbia has the right and the responsibility to determine how our public funds are used. We have exercised that right, and we have carried out our responsibility, in accordance with the wishes of the vast majority of our citizens.

The legislation is sound. The decision is right.

DIVESTMENT WILL
HARM BLACKS

Mangosuthu Gatsha Buthelezi

The author is the Chief of South Africa's 6 million Zulus and the leader of their political arm called Inkatha. The Zulus are South Africa's largest black ethnic group.

Points to Consider

1. How would divestment harm both blacks and whites in South Africa?
2. What is the relationship between divestment and revolutionary violence?
3. Why will armed struggle against apartheid fail?
4. What is the relationship of South Africa's economy to the economies of Southern Africa?

Excerpted from a memorandum presented to Prime Minister Shimon Perez of Israel in Tel Aviv, August, 1985.

The disinvestment campaign is not only detrimental to the interests of Black South Africans, but ultimately detrimental to the interests of Blacks in the whole of the sub-continent.

Those who are attempting to alienate South Africa from the international community are gravely mistaken. The more South Africa is alienated from the Western industrial democracies of the world, the more immune it will be to the kind of pressures which we need in the Black struggle. The total economic and political isolation of South Africa is sought by those who have declared their commitment to the armed struggle, and by those who seek to make the country ungovernable through the employment of violence. White South Africans cannot be punished into submission and the international community must realize that the need is not to punish White South Africa, but to strengthen Black South Africa in its democratic, non-violent demands for change.

Sharing Wealth

Apartheid has excluded the majority of Blacks from any meaningful participation in the country's free enterprise system. The massive industrial development that has taken place in the country has primarily benefited Whites, and it is this fact which makes people blind to the reality that Black South Africans do not want the wealth now monopolized by Whites to be destroyed, they want rather to share the benefits of the wealth that is produced by the country. All those who lobby to support disinvestment as a tactic and strategy ignore the fact that Black South Africans are fighting for their portion of what is already a thin slice of bread. A redistribution of the total wealth of South Africa would only destroy any prospects of progress. We need the redistribution of opportunity to create wealth, and we need the redistribution of opportunity to benefit from wealth, but to take away the slice of bread which Whites are claiming as their own because they refuse to share it, is to take away from both Black and White.

123

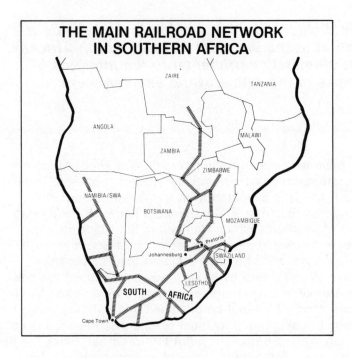

THE MAIN RAILROAD NETWORK IN SOUTHERN AFRICA

Black South Africans are entitled to a fair share of the wealth of the country because they contribute their share in the production of that wealth. But to destroy the prospects of creating wealth is to destroy all prospects of every having the future we are striving for.

The South African economy is indivisible. You cannot damage one portion of it without it having repercussions throughout the whole economy. Disinvestment, whether it be selective disinvestment or blanket disinvestment, will damage the prospects of the growth of the economy. Every Government of Western industrialized countries knows the extent to which economies are only minimally controllable. They cannot be switched on or off at will. The pace of economic development cannot be regulated at will. Economic growth is accumulative and Western observers should understand that while there may be a limited utility in the threat of economic sanctions against South Africa, the actual implementation of the disinvestment campaign would be useless unless it hurt the economy, and if it hurt the economy, Blacks now would suffer far more than Whites.

Leadership Division

The divide between Black South African leaders who champion the disinvestment cause and who reject it is a fundamental divide between protest politicians and politicans urging the use of violence for political purposes, and politicans working for non-violent means for bringing about radical change. I know of no mass meeting of Black South Africans which has given any Black leader a mandate to work for the economic downfall of the country. No Black grass root organization of any magnitude has ever supported disinvestment as a strategy Black South Africa would endorse. Thousands of thousands of Blacks wait outside factory gates for vacancies they hope to fill. Blacks already in employment do not abandon their employment to support the disinvestment lobby. Unquestionably, disinvestment will lead to ever-heightening levels of Black unemployment.

The Armed Struggle vs. Non-Violence

The African National Congress' Mission-in-Exile is working to destroy the country's economy. They are advising Black South Africans to sabotage the machinery of production, and they are seeking to create the kind of chaos in which the country will become ungovernable. If they succeed, they will not make it ungovernable for the National Party only. They will make the country ungovernable for subsequent governments for a long time to come.

Quite apart from these kind of considerations Inkatha's leadership realizes that we cannot win the struggle for liberation through an armed struggle and that we will have to use non-violent, democratic means of bringing about radical change. We also realize that it is well-nigh impossible to mobilize Black communities into effective opposition for the politics of negotiation if they are totally demoralized by mass poverty and the want and disease which accompanies it.

There is now a total interdependence between Black and White in South Africa and this interdependence is beginning to create the circumstances in which the politics of negotiation is favored. The stimulation of the South African economy into maximum possible growth rates is urgently needed to develop Black bargaining powers in a situation in

Sanctions and Disinvestment

I should like to draw attention to the inevitable consequences of the sanctions and the disinvestment measures on the agenda of the United States Congress.

It is impossible for the United State to impose punitive measures against South Africa only. They will be imposing these measures against the whole of Southern Africa. And who will they be hurting in the first instance?

Clearly the Black people of South Africa. This is common knowledge and has already been amply underlined, most effectively by Blacks themselves.

South African Dept. of Foreign Affairs, September, 1985

which they become ever-increasingly indispensible for the production of wealth. This is not just a vague generalization. It is a pertinent political statement of the fact that the upward vertical mobility among Black South Africans generates the kind of forces which accumulate to broaden bargaining bases. The greater the stake Blacks have in the economy, the more bargaining power they will have. Economic expansion from now onwards must necessarily ever-increasingly have vital spin-off benefits for Blacks. The economy has reached the point when any future expansion must necessarily draw substantial numbers of skilled workers out of unskilled ranks, and draw foremen out of skilled workers, and draw managers out of foremen. The ever-increasing upward vertical mobility of Blacks will weigh the scales in favor of the politics of negotiation.

There are existing backlogs which even the most enlightened Government could not eliminate within the foreseeable future unless economic expansion takes place at an unprecedented rate. Any damage to the real potential growth rate of the economy wil push the prospects of eliminating these huge backlogs into the unforeseeable future.

Economic sanctions have not worked anywhere in the world, and while Western governments are entitled to express their indignation about apartheid in South Africa in ways and means they see fit, they must be made aware that if they express indignation by applying economic sanctions against South Africa, they act in callous disregard of the wishes and the well-being of ordinary Black peasants and workers.

Southern Africa

There is generalized poverty across the whole of Southern Africa. Mocambique is now facing mass starvation in the foreseeable future. Every neighboring State depends for survival on the spin-off benefits of the South African economy. Inkatha's leadership is aware that the disinvestment campaign is not only detrimental to the interests of Black South Africans, but ultimately detrimental to the interests of Blacks in the whole of the sub-continent. Southern Africa is a natural economic universe in which interrelated and interlocked economies desperately depend on the generating capacity of the South African economy being steadily increased. The industrialization of the whole sub-continent depends on ever-increasing industrialization in South Africa. South Africa is a development base for the whole of the subcontinent and it is only those who indulge in pipe-dreams of socialist and communist Utopias who regard the present South African economy, based on free enterprise and integrated with Western industrial countries, as something which can be made a handmaiden to ideological designs.

It is tragic that I express the truth when I say that the disinvestment issue has ever-increasingly become a party political football in Western democracies. It is the Republican/Democrat confrontation in the United States which has dragged the disinvestment debate into the American political arena. There is genuine American disgust with apartheid, and there are those who naively think that support for disinvestment will assist the Black struggle for liberation, but prominent Americans who have had years of personal exposure in the political arena cannot claim to have this naivety. Western Governments owe it as a duty to South Africa and to Black South Africans to keep the disinvestment debate out of their party political arenas.

EXAMINING COUNTERPOINTS

This activity may be used as an individual study guide for students in libraries and resource centers or as a discussion catalyst in small group and classroom discussions.

The Point

Three-quarters of all South African Black production workers are firmly opposed to boycott and disinvestment as a "strategy for advancing Black liberation," but only nine percent favour not permitting American factories to function here under any circumstances.

This was revealed in a recent authoritative survey conducted by Professor Lawrence Schlemmer, head of the Centre of Applied Social Sciences at Natal University, which was commissioned by the American State Department. (South Africa Government, January, 1985)

The Counterpoint

A broad survey of 800 Blacks in 10 major cities was conducted several weeks earlier by the Institute of Black Research and the Community Agency for Social Enquiry. Confirming other recent polls that indicate mounting Black support for economic sanctions against the apartheid regime, this survey found that 73 percent of those questioned backed the call for a withdrawal of foreign investments from South Africa. The London *Sunday Times,* in a poll conducted in August, found 77 percent support for divestment. Ernest Harsch, *Intercontinental Press,* October 21, 1985)

Guidelines

Social issues are usually complex, but often problems become oversimplified in political debates and discussion. Usually a polarized version of social conflict does not adequately represent the diversity of views that surround social conflicts.

1. Examine the counterpoints above. Then write down other possible interpretations of this issue than the two arguments stated in the counterpoints above.

2. How do you interpret the cartoon by Richard Wright?

CHAPTER 4

THE U.S. AND SOUTH AFRICA

21 THE U.S. AND SOUTH AFRICA

CURTAILING EXPORTS TO SOUTH AFRICA

Thomas Conrad

Thomas Conrad is a staff researcher for the American Friends Service Committee (AFSC). The AFSC is a Quaker organization which strives to promote justice and disarmament in the United States and other nations.

Points to Consider

1. How do high-tech equipment sales in South Africa help to maintain apartheid?
2. Why are computers essential in the apartheid system?
3. What support have U.S. companies given to the South African police and military services?
4. What kind of export controls are recommended?

Excerpted from testimony by Thomas Conrad before the House Foreign Affairs Committee, February 9 and December 2, 1982.

The AFSC believes that economic pressure on South Africa to end apartheid must go far beyond the embargo. Based on the principle of rejecting profits from apartheid, the AFSC refuses to invest in firms with subsidiaries in South Africa and we encourage others to do likewise.

The United States has pledged to observe the international arms embargo against South Africa, first enacted in 1963 by the United Nations and made mandatory in 1977. In 1978, the U.S. government extended its restrictions on sales to South Africa. Broadly and generally speaking, the regulations prohibited the export to South Africa of any weapons—even those for private use—and all items on the Munitions List; banned sales of any commodities to the police and military; subjected certain dual-use items to special reviews; and applied the same restrictions to re-exports of U.S. origin commodities from third countries to proscribed end-users in South Africa.

While these regulations represented a step in the right direction, they were fraught with loopholes and blindspots that undermined the embargo; furthermore, they have apparently not been adequately enforced. In 1981, the Reagan Administration further weakened the embargo by lifting the ban on sales of airport safety equipment and medical supplies to military and police agencies. . . .

For the first time in several years, just recently South African magazines have again begun to carry advertisements for U.S. weapons.

One arms dealer's ad in a recent issue of the military magazine *Paratus* features Colt police revolvers and Remington riot shotguns. Another ad lists Winchester semi-automatic shotguns, Winchester pump-action riot guns, Smith and Wesson revolvers and Colt Army revolvers. Ammunition from Winchester, Federal and Remington are also available on the market in South Africa, according to the ads.

The continued availability of U.S. weapons in South Africa raises serious questions about the effectiveness of the embargo: How are these weapons reaching South Africa?

Who is responsible for exporting them? Is the U.S. government aware of this apparent violation? Will the government move to stop transfers of this kind?

While the export of actual weapons may be the most dramatic violation of the embargo, an equally serious and alarming problem is the failure of the embargo to adequately restrict the export of a vast range of critical technology and know-how including computers, electronics and communications gear, and information about these types of products. Although exports in this category are generally considered "non-lethal", many of them have direct military application. In all likelihood, the flow of high-tech equipment to South Africa is much larger than the flow of weapons. In the long run, exports of this type are probably more significant and pernicious than trafficking in actual arms because they contribute to South Africa's entire infrastructure of repression. . . .

As we see it, questionable high-tech exports to South Africa fall into three general categories: 1) those which clearly violate the embargo; 2) those which manipulate loopholes in the law that should be closed; and 3) those which however morally repugnant they may be—are legal but should be halted because they support apartheid and are inconsistent with the spirit of the embargo.

Support for Government Agencies

It is difficult to get any but the most general type of information about the sale of high-tech equipment to South Africa and how it is used there. A great deal more investigation is needed. However, even based on our limited inquiry in this area, we can show that numerous exports to South Africa from U.S. corporations contradict the arms embargo and directly involve the United States in administration of white rule. Several examples bear this out.

For several years IBM has knowingly rented a Model 370 computer system to the South African Department of the Interior which is used for the regime's national identity system. The IBM machine stores files on seven million people the regime has designated as "coloureds", Asians and whites. Information on blacks is stored on another computer. Since IBM owns the equipment and leases it to the government, it could withdraw from the arrangement, but has

Reprinted with permission of the *Minneapolis Star and Tribune*

declined to do so. Despite the fact that the IBM-based system helps facilitate the scheme of racial classification that apartheid is based on, the embargo has had no effect on this transaction. . . .

Local government bodies, as well, rely on computers from U.S. manufacturers. In many cases, U.S. corporations are supplying computer hardware to the very same agencies that are responsible for the legally enforced indignities inflicted on blacks, Indians and Asians who live in official white areas. The white-run government in Boksburg has an entire computerized municipal administration system based on a Univac machine from Sperry. NCR, which has played a strong visible role in computerizing white-run local governments in South Africa, has provided hardware to Pietersburg, Stellenbosch, Rustenburg and other cities. Mohawk has helped outfit Johannesburg and Germiston with hardware. IBM machines are used in Pinetown, Randfontein, Richards Bay and at the Pretoria "Peri-Urban Areas Board".

Sales to the overwhelming majority of South African government agencies do not fall under the U.S. ban. This loophole, we believe, is a major flaw in the embargo.

Support for South Africa's Police

Other evidence we have gathered indicates that the South African Police have continued access to U.S. technology and know-how in spite of the arms embargo. . . .

In 1978, after U.S. export controls were tightened, disk drives made by Control Data Corporation found their way into the hands of the South African Police as part of nine high-speed computers. Control Data's subsidiary in the United Kingdom sold the subunits to its business partner, ICL, which then built them into the larger processors destined for the South African police. Control Data insists that its sales to ICL are in compliance with U.S. law. ICL acknowledges using many components from U.S. producers in its computers. Since ICL is a major supplier of the South African military and police, there is reason to believe that thousands of dollars of U.S. technology are reaching embargoed agencies in South Africa via manufacturers in third countries. This matter has been the subject of a Commerce Department investigation for three years.

In 1979, RCA began exporting a radio system known as TAC to South Africa. The same system is used in the United States by police and businesses. A month after TAC was introduced to the South African market, a Johannesburg newspaper reported that the police were setting up an advanced new communications network covering the entire region around Johannesburg. Its name: TAC. RCA claims that somebody else outfitted the police with the equipment using the same name. The company insists that its hardware is not being used by the police and maintains that its exports to South Africa have all been legal. A representative of RCA acknowledged, however, that the company was not able to monitor how its equipment was being used within South Africa. The Commerce Department has started an investigation into the matter. . . .

Our survey indicates that many other kinds of security equipment from the United States are available in South Africa, despite the embargo. The list is too lengthy to detail here but it includes surveillance systems, sensors, devices to detect clandestine radio transmitters, security training packages and lie detector training. It takes little imagination to envision how commodities like these can be used as instruments of repression in the context of South Africa.

For most of the past five years, the U.S. has been South Africa's leading trade partner, U.S. companies supplying about 15% of its imports and absorbing about 8% of its exports. The 2-way trade amounts to about $4 billion a year almost evenly divided between exports and imports. This year it has been surging in both directions, as the U.S. recovery spurred demand for South African minerals and metals and the drought in South Africa required huge and highly unusual imports of U.S. corn.

Anna DeCormis, *Guardian,* December 26, 1984

Support for South Africa's Military

The Commerce Department's 1978 controls banned the export of any commodity "for delivery directly or indirectly to or for use by or for military or police entities. . ." Prior to this restriction, IBM had supplied the South African Defence Force with at least four large computers. IBM says that it has not sold any new machines to the military since the 1978 restrictions but a loophole in the embargo allows IBM and other U.S. corporations to provide maintenance and spare parts for military installations as long as these commodities don't originate in the United States. . . .

IBM claims these transactions are legal and insists that the firms do not use its products for military-related work. However, it is virtually impossible to determine how U.S. technology is actually put to use once it is out of the control of the companies who sell it. As long as the law allows U.S. subsidiaries to service military installations under "pre-embargo commitments" and to sell equipment and know-how to local companies that have links to the military, the embargo will be ineffective.

U.S. firms not only are involved in servicing and furnishing spares for existing military installations, they have also been supplying new technology to South Africa's military establishment:

In August 1979, it was revealed in the United Kingdom that computers made by the Massachusetts-based Digital Equipment Corporation were sold to the South Africans as part of a sophisticated radar system manufactured by Plessey, a British arms-maker. Furthermore, the Foreign Office confirmed that South African Air Force personnel had been trained on the hardware in Britain. In April of 1981, Plessey sent a follow-on shipment of air defense equipment to South Africa, which may have contained U.S. technology. Despite repeated requests, the U.S. government has refused to supply details of these transactions or to announce that any action has been taken to stop them. Such re-exports of U.S. products from third countries are supposed to be covered by the embargo. However, this case and others similar to it indicate that the United States has far to go in enforcing the embargo.

U.S. Army Collaboration

In addition to corporate transfers of U.S. military-related products and technology, the U.S. Army has been involved in an ongoing joint research program with a state-owned laboratory in South Africa. The program, which began a few years ago, has been continued under the Reagan Administration. We first became aware of the program when South Africa's National Physical Research Laboratory (NPRL) publicly acknowledged the cooperation of the U.S. Army Armament Research and Development Command (AARADCOM) in the Laboratory's most recent annual report. . . .

A research scientist at AARADCOM's Applied Physics Branch who works on the project confirmed that many of his experiments have been conducted in conjunction with researchers at the NPRL's High Pressure Physics Division, with whom he shares information regularly. He characterized the work as basic research on the behavior of certain metals when they are subjected to extreme pressure, and indicated that the goal of AARADCOM's work in this field was to develop a material that can be added to propellants to reduce the residue left in a firing chamber after a projectile is fired, a substance, as he explained in lay terms, that will cause a "self-cleaning out of gun tubes". The Army researcher maintained that his collaboration with the South Africans did not involve the actual application of his experiments, but it appears that results from the U.S. Army's work could easily be transferred to the development of ordnance in South Africa.

This collusion is not only objectionable on moral grounds because of its potential for South Africa's war machine: it also appears to be a serious breach of U.S. law. . . .

Conclusion

Is the U.S. arms embargo against South Africa working? From all appearances, it is at best an occasional and very mild irritant to the apartheid system. Now is not the time to consider softening the arms embargo against South Africa. We believe the United States should move to end all forms of collaboration with South Africa which bolster the apartheid state, or contribute to its internal security apparatus or military potential.

The AFSC believes that economic pressure on South Africa to end apartheid must go far beyond the embargo. Based on the principle of rejecting profits from apartheid, the AFSC refuses to invest in firms with subsidiaries in South Africa and we encourage others to do likewise. . . .

To address the problem of high-tech exports to South Africa is to confront a confusing array of hardware, electronics systems and technical specifications, a world devoid of human spirit. However, we cannot allow the question of the arms embargo to stay at the level of mere technology. We must never lose sight of how our technology effects the lives and aspirations of the people of southern Africa: A simple off-the-shelf electronic component can help guide a deadly missile toward its human prey. . .An automated requisition and rail transport system based on U.S. computers can help insure the bondage of Namibia by keeping South African forces there equipped with weapons and ammunition. . .U.S. made night vision equipment and computers can be used to track down Pretoria's political opponents and keep South Africa's blacks subjugated. . . .

We believe the United States is morally obliged to oppose the wholesale victimization of South Africans by apartheid, and to press for democratic rule. Therefore, we urge that U.S. export policy be realigned so it will be consistent with these goals.

22 THE U.S. AND SOUTH AFRICA

TRADE RESTRICTIONS ARE COUNTER-PRODUCTIVE

John H. Chettle

*John H. Chettle is the Director for the South Africa Founda-
tion in North and South America. Mr. Chettle describes the
Foundation as a private non-profit organization representing
a cross-section of races and economic interests in South
Africa that are interested in peaceful change and progress.*

Points to Consider

1. Why did South Africa build its own arms industry?
2. What effects does the arms embargo have on sales by
   American companies?
3. Why do African nations trade with South Africa?
4. What effects do trade restrictions have on reformers in
   South Africa?

Excerpted from testimony by John H. Chettle before the House
Foreign Affairs Committee, February 9 and December 2, 1982.

Restrictions serve only to weaken and undermine the moderate center, which argues that South Africa's historical destiny is to be aligned with the West.

We believe that the Foundation has been a catalyst in the process of change and reform in South Africa, and we try, as truthfully and objectively as we can, to reflect to those outside the country what is happening within it. . . .

Fortunately or unfortunately, depending on one's perspective, it is not easy to obtain meaningful results in foreign policy with trade restrictions.

Indeed, the chief effect of these actions has been to cause South Africa to build a formidable arms industry of its own, which now exports arms to a number of countries around the world; to reduce still further the leverage of the United States; and, as former Secretary of Commerce Philip Klutznick recognized in his annual summary of the restriction in 1979, to further "South Africa's determination to achieve economic self sufficiency and independence from any one foreign supplier", and to enable the major trading adversaries of the United States to be active " in turning the U.S. restrictions into strong points for their country's manufacturers."

Edward Banfield of Harvard has written brilliantly about the unintended consequences of government action. I am afraid that the main unintended consequences of the action taken by the Carter Administration are that they have harmed the United States by reducing its influence, reducing its trade, and reducing its reputation for reliability as a supplier. In the single area where we clearly have suffered from the embargo, that of seapower, they have also seriously affected our ability to be a useful ally of the United States if there were a conflict in which the Cape Sea Route was of strategic importance. . . .

Effect of Restrictions

The trade embargo on police and military equipment was introduced by the Carter Administration in February 1978, without any effort to seek public comment before it was issued. At the time there were no statutory criteria for the

Relaxing Siege Mentality

Our conscious effort to relax the siege mentality no doubt played a part in enabling then Prime Minister (now State President) P.W. Botha to take the bold decision to put forward constitutional proposals which cost the National Party one-third of its core Afrikaner constituency and gained it new white voters beyond Afrikaner ranks.

Chester A. Crocker, U.S. Assistant Secretary for African Affairs, January, 1985

institution of foreign policy based export controls. The language of the statute was both sweeping and vague. It prohibited the export to South Africa or Namibia of any commodity or non-public technical data whatsoever where the exporter "knows or has reason to know" that the item will be "sold to or used by or for" "military or police entities" in these destinations, or used to service equipment "owned, controlled or used by or for" such entities. Thus it has no limitations as to the categories of products or technical data. In the case of technical data, it further banned exports if the exporter "knows or has reason to know" that "any product of the data" will be sold to or used by or for police or military entities or service equipment owned, controlled or used by them. Finally, it bars re-exports to South Africa and Namibia of U.S. origin goods and technical data in third countries if the circumstances are such that direct exports would be banned. Thus, the incorporation of a single spark plug of U.S. origin in a car manufactured in Britain by a British owned firm which there is "reason to know" will be "made available for use" by some police unit in South Africa would be a violation of the embargo justifying the imposition of sanctions such as the denial of the right of the British firm to trade with the United States.

One of the least defensible aspects of this policy has been the application of it to products made in foreign countries and containing U.S. parts. The department has construed the provisions as barring foreign companies from exporting their products to police and military entities in

South Africa if there is even the smallest part of U.S. origin. This has led not only to poor relations with such countries but also led them to purchase parts from suppliers other than the United States. Moreover, while the United States is not in a position to give adequate surveillance to such proposals, they serve to damage U.S. firms who comply with the law. . . .

We estimate conservatively, that, in the 19 years since the unilateral arms embargo was imposed the United States has lost more than 14 billion dollars in trade with South Africa and some three quarters of a million jobs in the United States itself. These losses have occurred in the sale of defense and nuclear power station equipment alone. One wonders how many thousand jobs in Michigan, in New York and in California may have been lost as a result of such action. And this does not even begin to deal with the question of how much business was lost in the non-defense area.

Business Week reported on April 20, 1981 that Burroughs Corporation, for example, "could not get approval from Washington to export an electronic patient monitoring system for military hospitals and had to withdraw from competition for the million dollar contract. It went to Siemens, which also grabbed a $600,000 order for electronic medical equipment from Hewlett-Packard Co."

Not only were these jobs lost, but, as *Business Week* also reported, "The restrictions have proved a bonanza to European companies—and in particular to companies with high technology products—which wasted no time exploiting the opportunity. Siemens, for example, in 1976 was in the midst of dismantling its marketing effort for computers and other advanced electronics equipment, because the U.S. had a lock on the market. But when the Carter Administration acted, Siemens hurriedly reversed its pullout—and has since benefited handsomely."

Even more significant than that, however, is that actions of this kind—boycotts and restrictions—play into the hands of extremists on both sides—on the side of the extreme right-wing in South Africa, which argues that contact with the West will undermine the policy of apartheid; and on the side of the extreme left here and elsewhere, who see violent revolution as the only solution to South Africa's problems. Restrictions serve only to weaken and undermine the moderate center, which argues that South Africa's historical destiny is to be aligned with the West; who believe that South Africa must adapt its political system, not because the alternative would be international boycotts and sanctions, about which we are profoundly skeptical, but because it is the right thing to do; but who also believe that the West will not spurn South Africa's efforts to reform, and will recognize change when it comes. . . .

Africa's Growing Trade with South Africa

Even more to the point, South Africa's trade with black Africa is growing more rapidly even than its trade with the rest of the world, including the United States. In the three years between 1978 and 1980, South Africa's exports to black Africa doubled to more than $1 billion. South Africa is in fact the breadbasket of the region, supplying roughly 36% of Africa's maize and 18% of its wheat. 47 of the 53 African countries alone bought maize and wheat from South Africa in 1980. The South African *Financial Mail* reported that "South African canned food, wine and other products, labeled in English and Afrikaans, are found on supermarket shelves in Zaire, Malawi and Zambia. Armour plating for Zambia, police helmets for Uganda and fresh meat for Marxist Guinea have all been on Africa's shopping list." Zimbabwe imports three times as much from South Africa as from any other country and South Africa is the major market for Zimbabwe's exports. When the Queen opened the Commonwealth Conference at Lusaka, the red carpet on which she walked was flown up from South Africa for the occasion.

But in dealing with symbolism, the symbolism which tends so often to be forgotten is that of the symbolism of U.S. actions on reformers in South Africa. They have repeatedly to fight on two fronts. They must counter the opposition and obstruction of the extreme right-wing, which tries to prevent change at all costs, and they encounter the incomprehension and hostility of those who should understand their purposes abroad. All too often the "carrot" which is extended towards them consists merely in a cessation temporarily of beating them with the stick. Reformers, who have to cope with a situation of incredible complexity and delicacy, have a right to expect more understanding and sympathy from enlightened people abroad than they ever receive.

U.S.—SOUTH AFRICA
NUCLEAR COLLABORATION

The Washington Office on Africa

*The Washington Office on Africa is a non-profit organization
dedicated to the elimination of apartheid and the promotion
of racial justice.*

Points to Consider

1. How is Western nuclear collaboration with South Africa
   described?
2. What is the status of South Africa's nuclear weapons
   capacity?
3. Why does South Africa want nuclear weapons?
4. How has the United States helped South Africa gain a
   nuclear weapons capacity?

Excerpted from *Stop the Apartheid Bomb,* a publication by the
Washington Office on Africa, February, 1983.

U.S. corporations have also provided South Africa with the technology, equipment, materials and scientific training needed to create the Apartheid Bomb.

South Africa's acquisition of nuclear weapons capability is part of a larger picture of Western political, economic, technological, and military support for white minority rule. This support has strengthened the Pretoria regime as it has instituted increasingly sophisticated forms of repression and control over the Black majority population struggling for its liberation. The Apartheid Bomb marks a new era in Pretoria's military and political dominance in Africa.

History of Collaboration

Western nuclear collaboration with South Africa began in 1945 when Britain and the U.S. were searching for a reliable supplier of raw uranium for their nuclear weapons programs. Pretoria was the ideal partner with its vast uranium reserves in South Africa and occupied Namibia, and a cheap labor force of miners under tight, state control. The U.S. and Britain bought up all of South Africa's uranium and totally financed the development of its uranium mining and processing industries. Pretoria benefited immensely from huge revenues and increased Western reliance on its natural resources, and used these advantages to further its own nuclear program.

Washington was happy to oblige Pretoria's desire for its own nuclear industry. In 1957, as part of Eisenhower's "Atoms for Peace" program, the U.S. and South Africa signed an agreement whereby the U.S. provided South Africa with technical nuclear training, its first research reactor, SAFARI I, and the highly enriched, weapons-grade uranium to fuel it. (SAFARI I was completed in 1965 and the U.S. supplied South Africa weapons grade uranium for the reactor until 1976.) With this assistance, South Africa was able to build its own research reactor, SAFARI II, by 1967. The two reactors are located at the Pelindaba facility north of Johannesburg. ('Pelindaba' is a Zulu expression meaning 'We don't talk about this any more.')

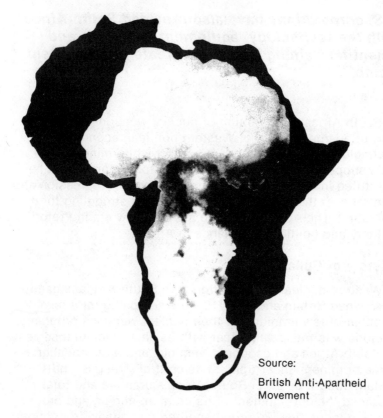

Source:

British Anti-Apartheid
Movement

Pretoria continued to expand its nuclear program—
including its ability to make nuclear weapons—by building
the Valindaba pilot uranium enrichment plant with U.S. and
West German assistance in 1975. ('Valindaba' means 'We
don't talk about this *at all.*') Later that year, Pretoria
announced its intention to build a large commercial enrichment facility with the hope of becoming a major enriched
uranium exporter in the 1980s.

In 1976, work began near Cape Town on building South
Africa's first commercial nuclear power reactor, Koeberg.
Built by the French consortium, Framatome, Koeberg is due
to start up in 1983.

South Africa's Nuclear Weapons Capacity

The Western countries attempt to justify their collaboration as assistance to South Africa's nuclear *energy* program.

South Africa designed that program to make it energy self-sufficient and able to resist an international oil boycott or other economic sanctions. Yet, "peaceful" nuclear power and nuclear weapons are just two sides of the same coin.

Nuclear reactor technology was originally designed to produce plutonium for nuclear weapons. As nuclear critic Amory Lovins has noted: "Nuclear reactors are essentially bomb factories that produce electricity as a byproduct." When the Koeberg power reactor is running at full capacity, it will produce enough plutonium to produce an atom bomb every two weeks. Furthermore, the SAFARI I research reactor already runs on weapons-grade uranium. While these two reactors are under International Atomic Energy Agency (IAEA) safeguards, many experts have noted the laxness of IAEA oversight, making diversion of materials for nuclear weapons possible if a government so chooses. Furthermore, South Africa has refused to sign the Nuclear Non-Proliferation Treaty or to submit its enrichment plant to any safeguards. Pretoria has already indicated Valindaba can enrich uranium to weapons-grade. In this context, there can be no *peaceful* nuclear collaboration with South Africa.

Why the Bomb?

South Africa hopes to gain great political and military benefits by simply *possessing* nuclear weapons and developing an extensive nuclear industry. Pretoria realized early on that its survival could be prolonged if it could create a greater Western dependence on its raw uranium supply and other natural resources. In addition, by *threatening* use of the bomb, Pretoria could effectively block international efforts to impose sanctions on it for its racist policies. Its politics of intimidation could also stonewall African support for the liberation struggle to eliminate apartheid.

South Africa has always seen itself on the frontline defending the West against communism, a view that most U.S. administrations have shared. If Western assistance continues, South Africa could develop and *use* tactical nuclear weapons as part of its "total strategy" to retain power. Pretoria might use such weapons on a neighboring country hoping to destabilize it or to weaken the liberation movements struggling for freedom. Or Pretoria might use the bomb on South African territory if it felt its hold on power

No Concessions

Despite growing fears that South Africa is pursuing a secret weapons program, the Reagan administration has not used its leverage to gain proliferation concessions. The Commerce Department has allowed the export of two powerful computers that would be invaluable in designing nuclear weapons. Commerce has also recommended congressional approval for the sale of helium-3 (which can be used to make the tritium needed in hydrogen weapons) and a hot isostatic press (which is useful for the metallurgy of bomb components). The Energy Department has also permitted U.S. companies to contract with South Africa for repair services at the Koeberg reactors.

Not Man Apart, *February, 1985*

was on the verge of collapse. As one Johannesburg lawyer told the *New York Times* in 1977: "As far as the Afrikaners are concerned, a South Africa that is not governed by them is not worth preserving."

Reagan and the Apartheid Bomb

Despite this overwhelming threat to the survival of the world, the Reagan Administration has *increased* nuclear assistance to South Africa by allowing exports of computers and other high technology goods to Pretoria's nuclear program. It has also negotiated with South Africa for the resumption of enriched uranium supplies, cut off when Congress passed the Nuclear Non-Proliferation Act in 1978, and allowed Pretoria to acquire needed enriched uranium from Europe through two U.S. brokering companies for its Koeberg reactor. This assistance is part of Reagan's "constructive engagement" policy designed to befriend Pretoria and provide it with increased economic, political, and military aid. Reagan has increased this nuclear assistance at the expense of deteriorating relations with Black Africa, which has repeatedly condemned the cozy relationship between Washington and Pretoria. The administration is not naive about Pretoria's nuclear weapons capability and how these exports strengthen it: in October 1982, a State Department spokesman concurred that South Africa has, or is "very close" to having, the bomb, and that Pretoria wants U.S. technology to assist it further. Just as the Reagan Administration spends billions of dollars increasing its nuclear arsenal at the expense of domestic social programs, so it openly supports the apartheid regime building its own nuclear arsenal at the expense of its Black majority, the African continent, and, perhaps, the whole world.

U.S. Companies are Crucial

Since the late 1940s, U.S. companies have helped maintain white minority rule in South Africa through aid to strategic sectors of its economy. U.S. loans have given South Africa crucial foreign exchange for making military-related purchases abroad. U.S. advanced technology, especially computers, has helped white South Africa control its majority Black population. Oil provided by U.S. companies has fueled its war machine.

U.S. corporations have also provided South Africa with the technology, equipment, materials and scientific training needed to create the Apartheid Bomb.

Why do U.S. corporations provide such direct support to a government known for its racist denial of basic human and democratic rights, and its high-risk potential for developing nuclear weapons? Why do they continue to violate U.N. Decree Number One (1979) which demands that corporations stop exploiting Namibian uranium and other natural resources until majority rule is attained?

A central reason for such collaboration is simple: profits! South Africa can afford to pay high prices for nuclear-related technology and offer high profits to U.S. investors because of the low wages and minimal health and safety standards it offers its Black workers. . . .

Those Black workers who mine uranium face unique health hazards working South African deep level and Namibian open pit mines. One Namibian uranium miner described his working conditions:

"Working in open air, under hot sun, in the uranium dust produced by grinding machines we are also exposed to the

*everpresent cyclonic wind which is blowing in this desert.
Consequently our bodies are covered with dust and one can
hardly recognize us. We are inhaling this uranium dust into
our lungs and many of us have already suffered the effect
. . . Our bodies are cracking and sore . . . There is no
hospital, bathing, swimming . . . or privacy and we are not
allowed to discuss matters of mutual interest."*

These inhuman conditions forced on Black Namibians and
South Africans have fueled growing Black protest. Black
labor unions are playing an increasingly central role in the
struggle for majority rule and greater social equity.

U.S. Corporations are Endangering Our Security

U.S. corporations have become more involved in South
Africa's nuclear industry as greater unionization and stricter
environmental laws have hit them at home. From the beginning, their involvement has been primarily a byproduct of the
U.S. nuclear weapons program and U.S. strategic interests
and it remains so.

The U.S. nuclear industry and its overseas activities have
reflected and shaped U.S. strategic goals around the world
since World War II. Those goals have placed concern about a
nuclear holocaust and social injustice second—at home and
abroad—to maintenance of U.S. military dominance and
unrestricted corporate access to "strategic" resources. A
major reason for U.S. cooperation in building the Apartheid
Bomb is to ensure unrestricted access to South African and
Namibian uranium and other strategic resources—regardless
of the human costs to South Africa's Black majority or to
U.S. Citizens.

U.S. corporations have helped South Africa, with Namibia,
become the third largest uranium producer in the world
(possibly the second by 1985). They have given South Africa
the know-how and materials to make nuclear weapons. They
have enabled South Africa to deter international pressures
for change and more effective support for the struggle for
freedom inside South Africa. By undermining non-
proliferation efforts, our government and corporations have
endangered our security while prolonging white minority rule
and encouraging Pretoria's continued military occupation of
Namibia. Can we afford to ignore this continued collaboration?

A NUCLEAR NON-PROLIFERATION POLICY

George Bradley

George Bradley made the following statement before a congressional committee in his capacity as the Principal Deputy Assistant Secretary for International Affairs, Department of Energy.

Points to Consider

1. What role does the department of energy play in the area of nuclear exports?
2. What nuclear exports are prohibited to South Africa?
3. What nuclear exports has the Reagan administration been permitting?
4. What "technical contacts" have been established with South Africa and what is their purpose?

Excerpted from testimony by George Bradley before the House Foreign Affairs Committee, February 9 and December 2, 1982.

In the case of South Africa, it has remained the firm U.S. policy that no direct exports of nuclear fuels and significant nuclear equipment to that country should take place unless and until it accepts full-scope safeguards.

I represent the Department of Energy (DOE) and I shall focus on the nuclear related aspects of the issue of U.S. export policy toward South Africa. I shall try to supplement the testimony that you are receiving from representatives of the Department of State, the Department of Commerce, the Arms Control and Disarmament Agency and the Nuclear Regulatory Commission and will focus my remarks on the specific questions that you addressed to Secretary Hodel in your letter of November 19, 1982.

In that letter you requested DOE's comments on a number of topics. You requested that we describe the Administration's current nuclear export policy towards South Africa and DOE's involvement in the approval process for nuclear exports. . . .

Policy Framework

The Department of Energy has important responsibilities in the fields of nuclear exports and nuclear weapons, non-proliferation policy development and implementation and civil nuclear cooperation. Few areas have been more difficult or required more attention. DOE is the agency that provides uranium enrichment services and that controls transfers of nuclear technology to other countries. We also assist the Department of Commerce in reviewing proposed exports of dual use items from the standpoint of their nuclear non-proliferation significance. We are actively concerned with nuclear non-proliferation policy formulation, including the support of international safeguards, and we have the lead responsibility for processing subsequent arrangements including approvals of retransfers of U.S. controlled special nuclear materials between cooperating nations.

We also support technological programs having international significance, such as U.S. efforts to substitute low for highly enriched uranium in research reactors. These are activities that affect several DOE offices besides International Affairs and I am accompanied here today by representatives of some of the other offices most involved. For example, our Office of International Security Affairs, in Defense Programs, is the focal point for reviewing Commerce export requests as well as implementing DOE's regulations that control transfers of unclassified nuclear activities outside the United States.

Non-Proliferation

The broad support for nuclear non-proliferation has been a key component in U.S. foreign policy for many years. As I understand your letter, the concerns you have expressed relate to:
- whether the Administration has changed its policy that South Africa adhere to the NPT (Non-Proliferation Treaty) and accept full-scope safeguards as a condition for obtaining U.S. fuel supply;
- whether the few export transactions that have occurred with South Africa in nuclear related areas are significant from a non-proliferation standpoint;
- whether we are making progress in our nuclear non-proliferation dialogue with South Africa;
- and whether current or future progress would be impaired or assisted if we were to move to an even more restrictive U.S. policy, namely, an absolute embargo on nearly all nuclear contacts and commerce with South Africa.

I shall respond to your concerns by outlining the current U.S. policy framework as I see it.

Reagan Administration

First, I believe it is important to stress that the current Administration is giving the same high priority to nuclear non-proliferation as has been given by previous Administrations. We believe that this is an area of foreign policy that must be approached in a bipartisan spirit. The Reagan Administration is a strong supporter of the NPT, of effective international safeguards and prudent export controls. While we have differed somewhat from those policies of the prior Administration which was somewhat hostile to certain aspects of the civil nuclear programs in Western Europe and

153

The Spirit of Nonproliferation

The Department is pleased to note that the chairman of the Atomic Energy Corporation of South Africa has announced today that the Government of South Africa will conduct and administer its external nuclear affairs in a manner which is in line with the spirit, principles, and goals of the Nonproliferation Treaty and the nuclear supplier's group guidelines.

U.S. Department of State, January 31, 1984

Japan, we have shared the view that exports to countries of nuclear proliferation concern must be approached with great caution.

Accordingly, in the case of South Africa, it has remained the firm U.S. policy that no direct exports of nuclear fuels and significant nuclear equipment to that country should take place unless and until it accepts full-scope safeguards and we have continued to urge South Africa to adhere to the NPT to achieve that objective. This is consistent with the policy and practice that was adhered to by the past two Administrations and I foresee no relaxation in the U.S. stance at this time. Relatedly, with reference to the questions that you raised in your November 19 letter about possible amendments to the NNPA (Nuclear Non-Proliferation Act), I do not foresee any near term efforts by the Administration to modify the provisions of Section 128 of the law so as to make that section no longer applicable to contracts prior to enactment of the NNPA. While there are aspects of the NNPA that obviously are less than ideal and that have created concern abroad, it is our current intention to live with the law and to avoid further, disruptive changes. . . .

Moreover, I expect the U.S. to continue to urge other nuclear suppliers to require "full-scope" safeguards as a condition of approving significant new exports to South Africa. This too is consistent with past practice. However, as you know, not all other suppliers share the U.S. view that insistence on such a policy is desirable in all cases since some believe that there may be instances where cooperation is desirable even if this test has not been met. . . .

So from my perspective, current U.S. non-proliferation policy towards South Africa remains as firm as it has been in the past and I believe it is erroneous to imply that we are dropping our guard. On the other hand, I do believe that our current willingness to talk to South Africa about our serious differences is producing some modest, but encouraging, results in the non-proliferation area.

Technical Contacts

In particular, in 1981, we reestablished technical contacts with the South Africans which, in time, might contribute to accommodations on the broader issues to which I have referred. I say this without any false illusions since I believe that we and the South Africans are still far apart on the NPT question. In particular, we exchanged visits and initiated technical discussions related to developing effective international safeguards for enrichment plants. Also, we initiated technical discussions on modifying research reactors to use fuels of lower enrichments. South Africa has established its own pilot enrichment plant at Valindaba and is building a larger enrichment plant to follow. Also, since it has been unable to acquire enriched uranium for several years from the U.S. it has successfully fabricated some of its own enriched uranium into fuel elements for its SAFARI research reactor.

From my perspective nothing is being lost in maintaining these contacts, plus there may be some gains, and I do not see how we can make progress unless we have some minimal contacts and some limited cooperation in non-sensitive areas. For this reason, I believe the complete legislatively mandated cut-off in contacts would be seriously harmful to our non-proliferation objectives.

Thus, while we are still very far apart from the South Africans on the fundamentals of joining the NPT, we, at least, are talking to them in the hope that our differences will narrow. . .

Further, I should note that in some respects the nuclear review and approach procedures that now are being proposed by the Administration as they apply to a nation like South Africa will be tighter than those that have previously been applied. . . .

Specifically, under the terms of our new regulations all transfers of unpublished, unclassified nuclear technology to non-nuclear weapon states that are not signators of the NPT or the Treaty of Tlatelolco and do not accept full-scope safeguards—such as South Africa—hereafter will have to be specifically authorized by the Secretary of Energy following coordination with State Department and consultation with the other interested agencies. Thus, even though the contacts between our two nations in the nuclear field are minimal we will have a better picture of non-governmental activities by U.S. persons to help assure that none of these activities contribute to any South African nuclear explosive activities. We also will be able to differentiate between transfers that appear warranted and those of greater sensitivity. Thus, more effective regulations will soon be in force.

U.S. POLICY
REINFORCES APARTHEID

John Conyers

John Conyers is a democratic representative in the U.S. House of Representatives from Michigan. He is a leading congressional critic of apartheid in South Africa.

Points to Consider

1. Why is South Africa an outlaw nation?
2. Why has "constructive engagement" failed?
3. What does Conyers mean by the policy he advocates called "constructive disengagement"?
4. How do South African blacks view U.S. policy?

John Conyers, "U.S. Policy Reinforces Apartheid in South Africa," *Detroit Free Press*, January 4, 1985.

In the eyes of the South African black majority, the entire African continent and indeed the entire world, the United States is now clearly viewed as collaborating with Pretoria in reinforcing apartheid.

South Africa: One of the world's most mineral-rich and aesthetically beautiful countries.

South Africa: The world's only country where a black majority of 24 million is constitutionally controlled by a tiny white minority of 4.5 million who deny blacks the right to vote; that can arbitrarily imprison, torture and execute them; that can forcibly evict and destroy entire communities; that can deny blacks pay, deny them the right to own property and even the right to object to this oppression.

South Africa: An outlaw country that illegally occupies its neighboring Namibia while launching military aggression throughout the entire region.

South Africa: a highly sophisticated police state now attempting to acquire nuclear weapons capability.

South Africa: A coming Armageddon.

Constructive Engagement

In 1981, the Reagan administration adopted a policy towards South Africa known as constructive engagement, which was based on the premise that closer ties with Pretoria and quiet diplomacy would be more effective in pressing for change. Four years of experience with this policy, however, have revealed it to be nothing less than systematized schizophrenia that gently criticizes apartheid with one hand, while feeding it with the other.

Indeed, constructive engagement has not only permitted the United States to be the largest trader and to become the second largest foreign investor in South Africa, but it has also stood as a toothless euphemism under which increased military, economic and political support to Pretoria have gone almost wholly unrestrained.

Despite the 1977 United Nations arms embargo, the Reagan administration has, under the auspices of constructive engagement, lifted restrictions on the export of military and police equipment as well as of nuclear technology to

"Hello, General Reagan? Send reinforcements quick!"

South Africa, allowing the sale of literally hundreds of millions of dollars of previously prohibited items. Those items include technology useful in the manufacture of arms, turbojet aircraft with intelligence-gathering capabilities, sophisticated computer equipment employed by the regime's security forces to maintain racial classifications and electric shock batons for use by the South African police.

In the name of constructive engagement, the United States has extended nuclear co-operation with Pretoria, despite its clear intention to acquire nuclear weapons capability and its refusal to sign the Nuclear Non-Proliferation Treaty.

The administration has licensed the sale of technology useful in developing nuclear arms and permitted the enrichment of South African uranium feedstock at three separate U.S. plants. It has refused to intervene when two U.S. firms brokered an arrangement to send enriched uranium to South Africa from France and it has exchanged official nuclear advisors with Pretoria.

Under the banner of constructive engagement, the administration has also given Pretoria economic aid and comfort with its unconditional support for a $1.1 billion International Monetary Fund loan in 1982, a year in which the South African mililtary budget increased approximately the same amount. In addition, the Reagan administration has expanded official intelligence contacts with Pretoria while repeatedly defending the regime in the face of United Nations condemnation.

Fruits of Constructive Engagement

And what are the fruits of this constructive engagement? Since 1981, South Africa has reinforced its structure of racial domination, accelerating the forced eviction from, and destruction of, black-owned communities—reassigning millions of blacks to overcrowded and impoverished camps and forcing three-fourths of the black majority to live on less than 13 percent of the land.

Pass-law arrests doubled between 1980 and 1982 and the arbitrary detention, imprisonment, torture and death of those who decry the system, such as Nelson Mandela, now in his 22d year of political detention, have increased dramatically. South Africa's illegal occupation of Namibia, and its widespread regional aggression have also escalated.

We must now recognize the perilous course that the administration's current policy is charting. If constructive engagement has succeeded in anything during the past four years, it has been in reinforcing the racial polarization and the pressures for a violent and bloody civil war.

Romance with Evil

We have attempted constructive engagement with apartheid, our "romance with evil" as it has been called. It has had its chance and failed. And the price for failure has been paid in the coinage of dead, dying, and imprisoned blacks in South Africa. The United States must now move on to play a different role, a role of activism and sacrifice, before the chance to negotiate is forever lost.

Senator Lowell Weicker, Speech at South African Embassy Protest, January 14, 1985

In the eyes of the South African black majority, the entire African continent and indeed the entire world, the United States is now clearly viewed as collaborating with Pretoria in reinforcing apartheid, in funneling there the actual tools of repression, in obstructing Namibian independence and in fomenting regional instability.

Constructive Disengagement

The United States must now move to a policy of what I would term constructive disengagement. This policy would first require the immediate termination of sales of military and police equipment, as well as nuclear technology, to South Africa, making it clear above all else that we are not the supporters and suppliers of the totalitarian and racist repression.

Second, the administration must adopt the anti-apartheid legislation that has received overwhelming support in the U.S. House. This package includes a ban on all new business investment and bank loans. It provides official support for UN Resolution 435, which calls for the immediate and unconditional South African withdrawal from illegally held Namibia.

It includes a ban on all sales of the South African gold coin, the Krugerrand, and a resolution calling for freedom for Nelson Mandela, leader of the Freedom Movement, and his wife, Winnie Mandela, who has also been detained under banning orders for nearly 20 years.Third, the administration must demand the release of all other political prisoners, withdraw the landing rights of South African aircraft in the United States and prohibit U.S. aircraft from landing in South Africa, ban the transfer and sale of all computer and nuclear technology and reimpose export controls relaxed during the past four years.

Such policy would make it clear to Pretoria that its continued intransigence on the matters of democratic enfranchisement and regional peace will be met with a strong and unequivocal response from the United States.

In the absence of demonstrable progress towards the elimination of apartheid within a specified timetable, constructive disengagement would then call for the gradual withdrawal of American companies from those sectors that directly fortify apartheid. U.S. firms now control 70 percent of the computer market, 45 percent of the oil industry and 33 percent of the automotive and truck market. Together, these sectors constitute the jugular vein of the highly sophisticated South African police state, without which Pretoria would have severe difficulty maintaining the racist political and economic structure.

Historical imperatives, as Nobel Peace Prize recipient Bishop Desmond Tutu has repeatedly pointed out, tell us that ultimately the black majority in South Africa will inherit its own land. When they do, they will remember who stood for them and who stood against them.

We must act now to avoid a coming Armageddon in South Africa and to assert ourselves on the side of the people in their struggle for sovereignty. Our national values and, indeed, our national interest so dictate.

PROMOTING PEACEFUL REFORM

George Shultz

Secretary of State George Shultz made the following comments in an address before the National Press Club.

Points to Consider

1. What approach has the Reagan Administration taken to influence change in South Africa?
2. Why is South Africa not a closed totalitarian society?
3. What progress has been made in race relations?
4. Why would it be a mistake for the U.S. to cut its ties with South Africa?

Excerpted from an address before the National Press Club on April 16, 1985.

There is now less cross-border violence than there has been in 11 years. There has been more reform in South Africa in the past 4 years than in the previous 30.

Today, I want to speak about an area of the world that has become a focus of interest and debate and where both our policies and the regional realities are too often misunderstood or even distorted. I am talking about southern Africa.

From the outset, the Reagan Administration undertook to help influence the process of change:
  • To accelerate the peaceful evolution in South Africa away from apartheid; and
  • To diminish the violence and instability that threaten lives and livelihoods throughout the region.
The complexities are daunting. But the United States has confronted an unsatisfactory situation, worked at the problem with care and determination, and achieved a good measure of progress. There have been ups and downs, obstacles and setbacks. But through painstaking diplomacy, we have reached the point where the agenda we proposed is accepted by all participants; where we, not the Soviet Union, have a major say in helping shape the region's political future. There is now less cross-border violence than there has been in 11 years. There has been more reform in South Africa in the past 4 years than in the previous 30.

The gains are fragile. Nonetheless, a process of change is clearly under way—offering hope to Africa's peoples if we continue to show responsibility and dedication in helping them manage that process.

South Africa

Let me start with the central issue of domestic reform in South Africa. In pursuing that goal, we have been guided by two important facts.

First, South Africa is not a closed, totalitarian society in which the government controls all aspects of life, all means of communication, all avenues of thought. While the white minority dominates the system, there is in that system a significant degree of openness of political activity and

164

President Botha inspects the President's Guard after delivering his inaugural address at the Parade in Cape Town.

Source: *South African Panorama*

expression—a generally free press, an independent judiciary, vigorous debate within the governing party and in parliament, and vocal critics of all viewpoints. There is nothing comparable in the Soviet Union. This degree of openness reflects the fact that white South Africa is not immune to the moral influence of the West; indeed, the white community's desire to be viewed as part of the Western world and its growing recognition of the need for change are among the grounds for hope for peaceful change. How many governments in the world would permit ABC's *Nightline* program to set up shop for a week, probe and dissect the country's ills, film heated debates between government leaders and their most ardent critics, and then show those programs to its people?

Second, we chose to focus on getting results. We cannot have it both ways: we cannot have influence with people if we treat them as moral lepers, especially when they are themselves beginning to address the agenda of change. South Africa's neighbors recognize this. We must, too.

By the same token, this has not kept us from speaking out—to South Africans of all races and to the American people. We have conveyed the message to the South African Government that a more constructive relationship with the United States is possible, *provided* that it demonstrates a sustained commitment to significant reform toward a more just society.

• We have consistently called for an end to apartheid.

• We have spoken out forcefully for press freedom and

against repressive measures such as forced removals, arbitrary detentions, and bannings.

•We have called for political dialogue between blacks and whites and for an end to Nelson Mandela's long imprisonment.

•With our support, U.S. businesses have become a positive force for change in South Africa by adopting the Sullivan code of fair labor employment practices and by providing educational, housing, and other benefits worth more than $100 million to their black employees over the past few years.

•We have developed nearly $30 million in assistance programs to train leaders in the black community to help them work more effectively for change in their own society.

Progress in South Africa

The truth is that South Africa *is* changing. For the most part, the transformation is being brought about by reality—by the growing realization that a modern industrial society simply cannot be governed by a preindustrial political philosophy of racial segregation.

The old illusion that South Africa's blacks could live permanently or enjoy citizenship rights only in designated tribal homelands—so that in the end there would no longer be any "South African blacks"—is being abandoned. Blacks are no longer prohibited from acquiring property rights in the supposedly "white" urban areas. The right of blacks to organize trade unions has been recognized, and black unions are now a powerful factor on South Africa's industrial relations scene; fully 50% of trade unionists in South Africa are black. Central business districts are being opened to black businessmen, and cities like Durban and Cape Town are desegregating their public facilities. Faced with the obvious injustice of forced removals of settled black communities and with the obvious inability to stop the influx of blacks into the cities, the government has suspended such removals and is shifting to what it calls an "orderly urbanization" policy.

The government has now acknowledged that it must consult with representative blacks about political participation outside the tribal homelands and at the national level; mere local self-government is understood to be inadequate. Just

Constructive Engagement

There are those in the United States and Africa who advocate punitive measures against and isolation of South Africa. . . .

I reject that approach, . . .

The prime focus of our efforts should rather be on positive steps to back constructive change and those in South Africa who are working for peaceful change. Constructive engagement is aimed at institution building and supporting those advocates of constructive change in South Africa of all races in and out of government.

Chester A. Crocker, U.S. Assistant Secretary for African Affairs, November 10, 1983

this week, the government accepted a special commission's report that calls for the abolition of laws banning interracial marriage and sexual relations—one of the most important symbols of apartheid.

If we recognize that white opinion holds vital keys to change, then we must also recognize that change must originate in shifts in white politics. In this regard, in the past 3 years, the white government has crossed a historical divide: it has been willing to accept major defections from its own ranks in order to begin to offer a better political, economic, and social deal to the nation's black majority.

These changes are not enough. South Africa is not now a just society. Serious inequities continue: repression, detentions without trial, and the prospect of treason trials for some black leaders. The issues of common citizenship for all and of black political rights have been raised but not yet concretely addressed by the government. The hated pass laws and influx control continue, though the government appears to be rethinking its actions on this front. Much more needs to be done. Change has just begun, but it *has begun.* Our job is to continue to encourage it.

The recent domestic violence is clearly a setback. All Americans are saddened and dismayed at the almost daily reports of violent encounters that have caused nearly 300 deaths among black South Africans over the past 9 months. The United States has consistently, repeatedly, and publicly deplored this bloodshed and the police tactics that only produce killings and add fuel to the unrest.

There is no excuse for official violence against peaceful demonstrators. Any government has a duty to maintain law and order. Nevertheless, that cannot be done simply on the basis of force; law and order also means due process and adequate channels for airing and resolving grievances.

But just as we recognize the right of peaceable assembly, so, too, if we are to be taken seriously, must we reject the right of any to take the law into their own hands. That is a formula for anarchy. We applaud the courage of those black leaders who press for nonviolent change, confronted on one side by a surging mass of black bitterness and on the other side by a long-unresponsive political system. . . .

There are also those who believe we should cut our ties with the Government of South Africa because of its racial policies. This is just as mistaken as the idea that we should refuse to deal with Angola and Mozambique because of their Marxist inclinations. We cannot bury our heads in the sand. We do not enhance our abililty to influence change in the region by eliminating ourselves as an actor.

Some propose that we try to cut South Africa off, to run it out of the Western world through boycotts, embargoes, and sanctions. They argue that even if such actions do not bring about change, our position will "put us on the side of right." I reject that view. It leads us down the road to ineffectual actions that are more likely to strengthen resistance to change than strengthen the forces of reform. It ignores the harm that such an approach will inflict precisely on the black majority whom the advocates of boycotts, embargoes, and sanctions purportedly want to help.

Opinion polls in South Africa by reputable organizations reveal that the overwhelming majority of black factory workers are *opposed* to disinvestment by American firms. . . .

The morality of a nation's policy must be judged not only by the noble goals it invokes but by the results and consequences of its actions.

If all Americans work together, this nation can be a major force for good. Thus, we serve our highest ideals.

INTERPRETING EDITORIAL CARTOONS

This activity may be used as an individualized study guide for students in libraries and resource centers or as a discussion catalyst in small group and classroom discussions.

Although cartoons are usually humorous, the main intent of most political cartoonists is not to entertain. Cartoons express serious social comment about important issues. Using graphic and visual arts, the cartoonist expresses opinions and attitudes. By employing an entertaining and often light-hearted visual format, cartoonists may have as much or more impact on national and world issues as editorial and syndicated columnists.

Points to Consider

1. Examine the cartoon in this activity.(see next page)

2. How would you describe the cartoon's message?

3. Try to summarize the message in one to three sentences.

4. Does the cartoon's message support the author's point of view in any of the opinions in Chapter Four of this publication? If the answer is yes, be specific about which reading or readings and why.

By Bill Sanders
(c) by and permission of News America Syndicate

BIBLIOGRAPHY
Southern Africa: Intraregional and U.S. Relations; Selected References

Bissell, Richard E. **South Africa and the United States: The Erosion of an Influence Relationship.** New York, Praeger, 1982. 147 p.

Cabaco, Jose Luis. "The Nkomati Accords." **Africa Report,** v. 29, May-June 1984: 24.

Chettle, John H. "The Law and Policy of Divestment of South African Stock." **Law and Policy in International Business,** v. 15, no. 2, 1983: 445-528.

Clough, Michael. "United States Policy in Southern Africa." **Current History,** v. 83, Mar. 1984: 97-100, 135-137.

"Cooperation in Southern Africa." **Africa Insight,** v. 13, no. 1, 1983: whole issue.

Crocker, Chester A., and Paul E. Tsongas. "Focus on Southern Africa: Constructive Engagement, Yes and No. **Foreign Service Journal,** v. 61, Feb. 1984: 25-33.

Davis, Jennifer, James Cason, and Gail Hovey. "Economic Disengagement and South Africa: The Effectiveness and Feasibility of Implementing Sanctions and Divestment." **Law and Policy in International Business,** v. 15, no. 2, 1983: 529-563.

Denoon, Donald, and Balam Nyeko. **Southern Africa Since 1800.** London, New York, Longman, 1984. 256 p.

Douglas, Carole A., and Stephen M. Davis. "Revolt on the Veldt." **Harper's Magazine,** v. 267, Dec. 1983: 30-41.

Frankel, Glenn. "Afrikaners: a Tribe Divided." **Washington Post,** July 29, 1984: A1, A18; July 30: A1, A22, July 31: A1, A10; Aug. 1: A1, A28.

Grundy, Kenneth W. **The Rise of the South African Security Establishment: An Essay on the Changing Locus of State Power.** Cape Town, South African Institute of International Affairs, 1983.39p.

Hansen, James. "High Strategic Stakes in Southern Africa." **National Defense,** v. 67, May-June 1982: 42-46; July-Aug.: 42-46.

Hill, Christopher R. "Regional Co-operation in Southern Africa." **African Affairs,** v. 82, Apr. 1983: 215-239.

Ispahani, Mahnaz Zehra. "Alone Together: Regional Security Arrangements in Southern Africa and the Arabian Gulf." **International Security,** v. 8, spring 1984: 152-175.

Jaster, Robert S. **A Regional Security Role for Africa's Front Line States: Experience and Prospects.** London, International Institute for Strategic Studies, 1983. 45 p.

_____ **Southern Africa in Conflict: Implications for U.S. Policies in the 1980s.** Washington, American Enterprise Institute for Public Policy Research [1982] 48 p.

Kitchen, Helen A., and Michael Clough. **The United States and South Africa: Realities and Red Herrings.** Washington, Center for Strategic and International Studies, Georgetown University, c1984. 48 p.

Liebenow, J. Gus. **SADCC: Challenging the "South African Connection".** Hanover, N.H., Universities Field Staff International, 1982. 15 p. (UFSI reports, 1982/no. 13, Africa)

O'Meara, Patrick. "South Africa: No New Political Dispensation." **Current History,** v. 83, Mar. 1984: 105-108, 131.

Parker, J.A. "Americanist editor J.A. Parker. **Review of the News,** v. 20, Feb. 8, 1984: 31-35, 37-38.

Price, Robert M. "Pretoria's Southern African Strategy." **African Affairs,** v. 83, Jan. 1984: 11-32.

Republic of South Africa. Dept. of Foreign Affairs and Information. **Economic Co-operation in Southern Africa.** Pretoria, 1981. 80 p.

Seiler, John. "Constructive Engagement in South Africa: A Viable U.S. Policy." **SAIS Review,** winter 1981: 161-168.

_____ "Policy Options in Namibia." **Africa Report,** v. 29, Mar.-Apr. 1984: 61-63.

Shultz, George P. "The U.S. and Africa in the 1980s." **Dept. of State Bulletin,** v. 84, Apr. 1984: 9-12.

Southern Africa Since the Portuguese Coup. Edited by John Seiler. Boulder, Colo., Westview Press, 1980. 252 p.

"Southern Africa's Drought: Nature's Curse, Man's Folly." **Economist,** v. 290, Feb. 11, 1984: 70-71.

U.S. Congress. House. Committee on Foreign Affairs. Subcommittee on Africa. Namibia and Regional Destablization in Southern Africa. Hearing, 98th Congress, 1st session. Feb. 15, 1983. Washington, G.P.O., 1983. 126 p.

_____ Regional Destabilization in Southern Africa. Hearing, 97th Congress, 2nd session. Dec. 8, 1982. Washington, G.P.O., 1983. 175 p.

_____ United States Policy toward Southern Africa: Focus on Namibia, Angola, and South Africa. Hearing and markup, 97th Congress, 1st session, on H. Res. 214; H. Con. Res. 183. Sept. 16, 1981.

U.S. Congress. Senate. Committee on the Judiciary. Subcommittee on Security and Terrorism. The Role of the Soviet Union, Cuba, and East Germany in Fomenting Terrorism in Southern Africa. Hearings, 97th Congress, 2nd session. Mar. 22-31, 1982.

"U.S. Policy toward Sub-Saharan Africa." **Orbis,** v. 25, winter 1982: whole issue.

Whitaker, Jennifer Seymour. "Africa Beset." **Foreign Affairs,** v. 62, no. 3, 1984: 746-776.

Additional Readings

Books

Carter, Gwendolen M. **Which Way is South Africa Going?** Bloomington, Indiana University Press, 1980. xii, 162 p.

Fredrickson, George M. **White Supremacy: a Comparative Study in American and South African History.** New York, Oxford University Press, 1981. xxv. 356p.

Gann, Lewis H. Duignan, Peter. **Why South Africa Will Survive: a Historical Analysis.** New York, St. Martin's Press, 1981. 312p.

Study Commission on U.S. Policy toward Southern Africa. **South Africa: Time Running Out.** Berkeley, University of California Press, 1981. xxviii, 516 p.

Articles

Barber, James. "Afrikanerdom in Disarray." **World Today,** v. 38, July-August 1982: 288-296.

Bowman, Larry W. "The Strategic Importance of South Africa to the United States: an Appraisal and Policy Analysis." **African Affairs,** v. 81, April 1982: 159-191.

Huntington, Samuel P. "Reform and Stability in South Africa". **International Security,** v. 6, Spring 1982: 3-25.

Legum, Colin. "The End of Apartheid." **Washington Quarterly,** v. 5, Winter 1982: 169-178.

Schlemmer, Lawrence. Welsh, David. "South Africa's Constitutional and Political Prospects." **Optima, v. 30, no. 4, 1982: 210-231.**